D0930113

HISTORICAL DEVELOPMENT OF THE
UNIVERSITY SYSTEM OF GEORGIA

Historical Development of the University System of Georgia: 1932-1990

CAMERON FINCHER

Institute of Higher Education
University of Georgia
Athens, Georgia

Preface

This brief book discusses the historical development of the University System of Georgia. No efforts have been made to write a comprehensive history of the Board of Regents, the various institutions that are now units of the University System, or the innumerable public issues and policy decisions that have been instrumental in the University System's growth and expansion since its inception in 1932. The intent is simply to tell how the University System has grown, developed, and progressed over a sixty-year period.

The historical development of the University System is more intelligible when discussed in terms of institutions, programs, and policies. To that end, many other stories have been carefully avoided. There is no desire or intent to write about personalities and politics; that is another story altogether and one that would distract greatly from the more significant and meaningful efforts to develop a comprehensive system of public higher education in Georgia. Neither is the story one of the Board of Regents, its individual members, and its policy-making procedures. That, too, is another story and one that cannot be told with sufficient accuracy and reliability to warrant publication. The annual reports, minutes, and other records of the Board of Regents are much too silent on the deliberations of policy and the influence of individual members.

Special care has been taken to "control" references to funding, financing, and budgeting. The search for adequate funds is a never-ending struggle in higher education and once introduced into a discussion, funding (like politics) dominates everything else that follows. Enough is said about annual budgets to show that funding is important, has never been adequate, and will always be a matter of intense concern. Enough has been said also to show that institutions of higher education can and do survive under financial adversity.

Another related matter that has been avoided is the legal issues of the past forty-five years. Legal issues and judicial process are often more dominant than finances and politics. Legal proceedings, in particular, lead to eventual resolutions of conflict but not to the solution of educational problems. After the judication of conflict it is virtually impossible to trace cause-and-effect relations in the midst of so many concurrent events and unanticipated outcomes.

This book would be more interesting if it could explain how public policy issues are resolved and how major policy decisions are made. Regrettably that story must be avoided like politics and funding, but not for the same reasons. Observation and study of "the process" will suggest that policy decisions are seldom made in public. The vast majority of policy decisions is not a matter of mere proposal and approval; such decisions are not disclosed in recorded minutes, published statements, or written policy manuals. Neither is a policy decision merely the exercise of personal power or influence, a matter of who decided what on which day! With respect to the public and institutional policies discussed here, it has been difficult enough to peg major policy decisions with a date.

Why then a book on the University System's historical development and *not* a history of the University System of Georgia? The reasons are fairly clear: the development of institutions, programs, and services in a complex, multi-purpose, statewide system of public higher education is never a matter of specific events, decisions, and actions; for the most part, such development is an extended process in which varied responses are made to the stimulus of public demands and expectations. The development of institutions, in particular, implies an internal differentiation and integration of structures and functions that often follow a schedule of their own. No one creates a university (or university system) by signing a charter, enacting a law, amending the constitution, or rendering a majority vote. The creation of such institutions is a developmental process that takes many years and the concerted efforts of many people. Thus, there are excellent reasons to believe that "historical development" is the appropriate term to designate what this book is all about. The development of the University System of Georgia began several years before the Reorganization Act of 1931, and it continues long after the Board of Regents attained constitutional status and authority.

Because of such reasoning, readers will find a pronounced emphasis on survey reports, committee recommendations, the work of outside consultants, and various public documents such as annual reports. Taken one at a time, they are a tedious form of literature; taken together they tell a story that all Georgians should appreciate. Dry and dusty reports often tell us what was missing "at the time," what was needed but not supplied, and what the next "stage of development" might possibly be. Many of these reports were written by observers with the best of intentions, but far removed from the pressures of policy and decision making. As a result, they were often able to see more clearly what needed to be done and how to do it. At other times, of course, they were professionally right but historically wrong.

The University System thus has grown and developed in response to public demands and expectations that changed as "the times changed." Institutions of higher education have been closed, merged, reorganized, planned, established, and appraised as social, economic, political, and cultural conditions changed for "better or worse." Programs of instruction, research, and service have prospered or struggled with changes in public and private support. *And* the units of the University System have responded with programs and services as public demands and expectations have changed with national, regional, and state trends.

In their responsiveness to changing demands, the colleges and universities of the University System have exceeded most reasonable expectations. In many respects and from many different perspectives the University System is the State of Georgia's most remarkable achievement and the finest thing that Georgians have ever done for themselves. As a statewide system of public higher education, the University System is exemplary; its progress has often been uneven and irregular, but its progress has been continuous and its development reflects a commitment to intellectual, technological, and cultural progress that is often missing in other areas of human endeavor. Georgians, like residents of other states, are occasionally inclined to boast; in the University System of Georgia they have accomplished something in which they can take genuine pride.

Cameron Fincher
August 1, 1991

Acknowledgments

The substance and style of this book have been influenced in many ways by Thomas W. Mahler (1917-1990), a professional colleague and personal friend for almost forty years. As administrative dean of the Atlanta Division of the University of Georgia, Tom Mahler hired me for my first job and gave financial assistance (as well as personal encouragement) in the continuance of my graduate education. He was most influential in my "transfer to the Athens campus," and I, like many others, continue to benefit from his insights, perspectives, and professional experience. When he retired as director of the Georgia Center for Continuing Education, he gave me his collection of the Regents' annual reports because he knew that I "would find them useful." I did indeed find them useful and acknowledgment here is the best way to dedicate this book to his memory.

A book of this kind is necessarily the outcome of many years of reading, thinking, discussing, and writing. It's impossible to acknowledge the many friends and colleagues who have contributed to my "reading, thinking, and discussing," — and so, it makes sense to concentrate on those who have given extraordinary assistance in the "writing." For her patient and conscientious preparation of camera-ready copy—Mrs. Susan Sheffield deserves all the words of appreciation that I can muster. Not only has she prepared the pages of text, but she has organized the maps showing the institutional growth of the University System over its sixty-year history. Mrs. Mary Snyder has diligently "proofed" two or more versions of the book and made numerous suggestions for the book's general improvement. Mrs. Joyce Placek has proofed, double-checked computations, and revised various estimates as the "writing" extended into a new academic year and encountered more recent data or information. Dr. Jim Hearn and Dr. Libby Morris incited many "last-minute" improvements in the text by their careful reading of the manuscript and their willingness to raise questions about ambiguous sentences and paragraphs.

All contributions considered, camera-ready copy has been prepared by the Institute staff using our desktop publishing capabilities; the maps have been prepared for printing by the University of Georgia's Cartographic Services Laboratory, and the book has been printed by the University Printing Department. As in all previous Institute publications, the finished product reflects the splendid cooperation that intra-campus agencies give each other at the University of Georgia.

Cameron Fincher
August 1, 1991

"We realize that this report is long, but believe that every word in it is necessary for you to reach an understanding of our problems. It has taken us twelve months to gain even a general knowledge of our Higher Educational Institutions, which should bear good fruit hereafter.

We state emphatically that it is not our purpose to aggrandize any institution without due regard to all of the others. It is, however, our plain duty to mold the institutions in the University System into an Educational System, in fact, as well as in name. It must comprise a group of separate institutions, under common control . . ."

—1932 Annual Report

Contents

List of Figures

CHAPTER ONE
Reorganization and Coordination: 1932-1943

*He who considers things in their first growth and origin
will obtain the clearest view of them.*

Aristotle, *Politics*

The University System of Georgia has developed gradually
and unpredictably since its inception in the early 1930s. The
System began in the interest of economy and under conditions
that were extremely adverse for education. As the System has
developed, it has overcome one adversity only to be set back by
another. Nonetheless, the life history of the University System
has been an appreciably steady, gradual, and continuous progression to its current status as an exemplary statewide system
of public higher education.

The authority and responsibility of the Board of Regents
have evolved in the midst of many legal, political, economic,
and social difficulties. The Constitution of 1877 (adopted in the
post-reconstruction era) provided for schooling in the "elements
of an English education only" and for "donations" by the general assembly to the University of Georgia. As a result of legislative short-sightedness, the development of both secondary
and higher education within Georgia was severely hampered.
No provision for state-supported high schools was made until
the early years of the 20th century when amendments to the 1877
Constitution allowed the general assembly to delegate the
levy of taxes for "educational purposes" to counties (Orr, 1950).

The movement for a centralized governing board for all
public institutions of higher education began in the 1920s as
part of a public demand for the reorganization of state government. Specific mention of a board of regents was made as early

1

as 1919 when Governor Hugh Dorsey (1917-1921), as chairman of the budget and investigating committee, stated:

> We are decidedly of the opinion that it would be in the best interest of our higher institutions of learning if a small Board of Control or State Board of Regents should displace the army of trustees now appointed largely by reason of political support. (p. 15)

In 1922 Governor Thomas W. Hardwick (1921-1923) commissioned a study of state government with specific mention that the State was "board-ridden, commission-ridden, and trustee-ridden." The General Assembly took no action on the recommendations of the consultants hired by Governor Hardwick, but public support for simplification and reorganization gained momentum five years later. In 1927 the Georgia League of Women Voters, the Institute of Public Affairs at the University of Georgia, and the Institute of Citizenship at Emory actively supported reduction of the State's ninety-plus agencies to twelve or fourteen departments. At that time the University of Georgia had 331 trustees for its various branches (Gosnell, 1936).

The report of a state survey committee, appointed in 1925 by Governor Clifford Walker (1923-1927) and chaired by C. Murphey Candler, stated that "possible friction or rivalry between the higher institutions and some duplication of work could be eliminated, and much better results for all obtained, if there were one Board of Trustees or Regents . . ." (p. 8). The committee added that proper safeguards should be involved in appointments and the alumni of no one institution should dominate.

In 1929 the Georgia Commission To Simplify and Coordinate the Operations of Governmental Departments was appointed by Governor L.G. Hardman (1927-1931) and chaired by Ivan Allen, Sr. The Commission recommended a department of state government to be known as the "Board of Regents of the University System of Georgia" (p. 23). The University System

Figure 1
ORIGINAL INSTITUTIONAL COMPOSITION OF THE
UNIVERSITY SYSTEM OF GEORGIA (January 1, 1932)

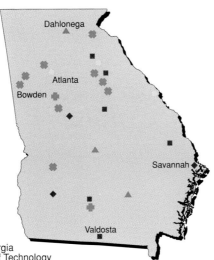

● **Universities**
University of Georgia
Georgia School of Technology
Medical College of Georgia

■ **Senior Colleges**
Georgia State College of Agriculture
  and the Mechanic Arts
Georgia State Teachers College
Georgia State College for Women
Georgia State Woman's College
Georgia State College for Men
South Georgia Teachers' College

✱ **A&M Schools**
4th District A&M School
7th District A&M School
8th District A&M School
9th District A&M School
10th District A&M School
Bowden State Normal
  and Industrial College
State Agricultural & Normal College
Georgia Industrial College
The Georgia Vocational & Trade School

▲ **Junior Colleges**
North Georgia College
Middle Georgia College
South Georgia College

◆ **Colleges for Blacks**
Georgia State Industrial College
Agricultural, Industrial & Normal School
State Teachers & Agricultural College

✱ **Experiment Stations**
Georgia Experiment Station
Georgia Coastal Plains Experiment Station

Cartographic Services Laboratory, University of Georgia

should consist of the University of Georgia and all its branches. The plan for reorganization was drawn up by Chairman Allen, Hooper Alexander, and Cullen Gosnell; the accompanying legislative bill was drafted by a committee of the Atlanta Lawyers' Club (Gosnell, 1936).

The bill for reorganization was defeated in the House by a vote of 109 to 81, but the essential features of the bill were revised by a legislative committee appointed by Speaker Richard B. Russell, Jr. and chaired by Hugh Peterson who had been a member of the Allen Commission.

When Russell was elected Governor (1931-1933), he repeated his pledge to reorganize state government. The Reorganization Act of 1931 quickly followed and with the abolishment of 53 state boards, commissions, and bureaus the powers previously vested in 27 boards of trustees were consolidated under a single Board of Regents (Saye, 1948).

The University System of Georgia became a legal reality on August 28, 1931 when Governor Richard B. Russell, Jr. signed an act of the General Assembly "To Simplify the Operations of the Executive Branch of State Government." The Board of Regents was officially organized on January 1, 1932, the first day of its existence, and consisted of eleven members appointed by the Governor who served as an *ex officio* member. Prominent members of the first Board were Cason Callaway, Martha Berry, Richard B. Russell, Sr., George C. Woodruff, and Philip Weltner. The first elected chairman of the Board of Regents was W.D. Anderson of Macon and the first appointed chancellor was Charles M. Snelling, former president of the University of Georgia. Philip Weltner was elected vice-chairman and Earle Cocke, Sr. was appointed secretary-treasurer.

The first Board of Regents thus consisted of eleven members, one each from the ten Congressional districts and one member at large who served at the pleasure of the Governor. Members of the Board were appointed by the Governor (with consent of the Senate) for four terms. They elected their own chairman and were authorized to select a secretary.

The Regents inherited from their several preceding boards of trustees financial difficulties. For the years 1929-1931, the Regents inherited outstanding debts of $1,074,415 and 26 institutions whose locations were "known only to a few" and whose operations were "known to no one person or group" (1932 *Annual Report*).

The institutions and agencies for which the new Board was responsible were an unbelievable array of senior and junior colleges, A&M schools, and agricultural experiment stations. From the various boards of trustees, the Regents inherited three university-level institutions located in Atlanta, Athens, and Augusta; five senior or four-year colleges located in Athens, Milledgeville, Statesboro, Tifton, and Valdosta; three junior colleges at Cochran, Dahlonega, and Douglas; eight district A&M schools (or their variants) in Barnesville, Bowden, Carrollton, Clarkesville, Granite Hill, Madison, Monroe, and Powder Springs; three colleges for blacks in Albany, Forsyth, and Savannah; and two agricultural experiment stations in Griffin and Tifton.

As shown in Figure 1, these various agencies had been scattered about the State in response to local needs, as perceived in the past, and in tune with the political pressures of the era in which they had been established. Only two of the agencies were located north of Atlanta and only one was located on the Georgia coast; none were located in the northwest and southwest corners of the State. Three of the institutions were located in Athens alone: the University of Georgia (1785), the Georgia State College of Agriculture and the Mechanic Arts (1872), and the State Teachers College (1895). The colleges for agriculture and education began as separate institutions and later became a branch of the University with their own presidents and trustees. Their complete integration within the University of Georgia would not be complete for eighteen more years.

Each of the 26 institutions began as a hopeful solution to the State's educational problems. The A&M schools were established in 1907 and 1908 as district high schools to meet the needs of rural areas. The schools were located in each congressional district *as* branches of the State College of Agriculture and *with* trustees as representatives of the included counties. Their programs were a mixture of manual labor and secondary schooling that was superceded by the growth of public high schools and by passage of the Smith-Hughes Act of 1917. By the mid-1920s the A&M schools had outlived their purpose and seven were converted to colleges by the state legislature. Descendants of four A&M schools would become Georgia Southern, Georgia Southwestern, South Georgia, and Middle Georgia colleges.

The three colleges for blacks began as the Georgia State Industrial College (1890) in Savannah, the Georgia Normal and Industrial College (1917) in Albany, and the State Teachers' and Agricultural College (1922) in Forsyth. The latter college would be consolidated in 1939 with the Fort Valley High and Industrial School (1895) to become Fort Valley State College. The two experiment stations were outgrowths of the Hatch Act of 1887 and were in 1932 independent state agencies with federal funding.

To cope with its 26 disparate institutions and their debts, the Board of Regents moved quickly to obtain $20,000 from the General Education Board for a comprehensive survey by "disinterested expert educators and economists." The objective of the survey was to make the University System "more efficient from an educational viewpoint and more economical from a taxpayer's point of view" (1932 *Annual Report*). The funded survey began in May, 1932 and was concluded in February, 1933. Members of the survey committee were: George F. Zook, president of the University of Akron; Lotus D. Coffman, president of the University of Minnesota; Charles H. Judd, dean of education at the University of Chicago; Edward C. Elliott, president of Purdue University; and George A. Works, professor of higher education at the University of Chicago (and chairman). The members of the survey committee were well respected educators and the survey they conducted was typical of national efforts to study and to improve the general condition of education beyond the high school.

Among the Regents' many accomplishments in their first year were the requirement of surety bonds for institutional deposits in local banks, the consolidation of all insurance for the separate institutions, the discontinuance of institution-owned automobiles, and completion of its first year *without* borrowing money. Despite receiving only 86 percent of its state appropriations for 1932, the Board reduced its indebtedness to $702,502.

Constructive measures were taken to integrate the three separate Athens institutions into one. Farms and dairies were combined, and all dining halls and dormitories were placed under one management. Policies were established whereby faculty salaries would be decreased proportionately to reductions in state appropriations. For 1932 this meant a 14 percent reduction in faculty salaries which was in addition to other reductions imposed to balance institutional budgets. The total reduction in institutional operations for the year was $507,739.

Policies were established whereby heads of institutions would handle all personnel grievances and settle other internal difficulties. The Regents would hear complaints only when other remedies had been exhausted and when appeals were "reduced to writing." The Regents heard only two appeals in 1932, both of which resulted in sustainment of the president's decision.

One institution, the 10th District A&M School at Granite Hill, was closed in 1932. Foremost among the Regents' recommendations to the Governor was authority to "consolidate institutions, suspend and/or discontinue their operation, merge departments, inaugurate or discontinue courses, abolish or add degrees." The reorganization of institutions would be less drastic if done by the Regents instead of the General Assembly. Given such authority, the Regents would eliminate institutions offering only high school work and remove secondary school-work from other institutions (with the exception of the three black institutions).

Also sought by the new Board was a single appropriation from the State *and* the authority to allocate and/or distribute such funds as the Regents saw fit. Some institutions had funds in excess of their necessities while others were in want. The state legislature did not have time to ascertain institutional needs, but the Regents did. In recommending a reduction of state appropriations in 1933 (from 1.9 million to 1.5 million dollars) the Regents demonstrated awareness of the State's financial depression but added that they could not operate on the lesser budget without the requested authority to re-organize.

Other recommendations made by the first Regents were: (a) a fiscal year beginning on July 1st and ending the following June 30th; (b) annual appropriations according to the new fiscal year; and (c) a special appropriation of $100,000 for repairs to buildings. The special appropriation for repairs was the only recommendation not honored by the state legislature.

In closing its first annual report, the Regents stated their commitment to an "Educational System, in fact, as well as in name" and their encouragement of "diversity of educational effort because of the diversity of human needs." The Regents, however, did not "subscribe to the idea of multiplying courses and taking on new fangled educational ideas because some great university, with millions of dollars of endowment funds, is experimenting in these fields." The Board did subscribe to "a sense of obligation to their State" on the part of students and the necessity of local pride giving way to the best educational interests of the whole State (1932 *Annual Report*).

A NEW UNIVERSITY SYSTEM

With the additional powers authorized by the State and the recommendations of its prestigious survey committee, the Board of Regents created in 1933 a strengthened system of senior and junior colleges. Relinquishing most of their responsibility for secondary schoolwork, the Regents closed A&M schools in Carrollton, Powder Springs, Madison, and Clarkesville, plus the Vocational & Trade School at Monroe. They discontinued high school coursework at South Georgia Teachers' College (in Statesboro), North Georgia, Georgia Southwestern, Middle Georgia, and South Georgia colleges but continued such work at the institutions in Savannah, Albany, and Forsyth.

State support for the Bowden State Normal & Industrial College was discontinued when West Georgia College (a junior college) was established in Carrollton. The Georgia State College for Men in Tifton was abolished and replaced by Abraham Baldwin Agricultural College. Senior college work was also eliminated at North Georgia, giving the State a total of eight two-year colleges (six for whites and two for blacks).

Seven institutions were classified as four-year institutions and included the newly merged University of Georgia (including the agricultural college and the normal school), Georgia Tech, Georgia State College for Women (Milledgeville), Georgia State Woman's College (Valdosta), South Georgia Teachers College (Statesboro), the School of Medicine (Augusta), and Georgia State Industrial College (Savannah). Creating the Evening School of Commerce (or Division of Adult Education of the University System of Georgia), the Regents added an eighth four-year institution and, with the two agricultural experiment stations, brought the total number of University System units to eighteen (1933 *Annual Report*).

In his 1936 annual report Chancellor S.V. Sanford announced that the reorganization of the University System had been completed and added that "no further changes are considered necessary." The 1936 annual report was the fifth from the Regents, the first to Governor E.D. Rivers, and the second to be written by Chancellor Sanford. It was also the first annual report to include photographs of buildings on the various campuses. Chancellor Sanford overlooked the role of the New Deal in the University System's "economic recovery" and addressed the more pressing educational issues facing the State's system of public higher education. Among the many educational needs recognized were: (a) more attention to guidance and counseling, (b) a graduate school of "high standing," (c) graduate work for teachers, (d) the demand for trained men and women in social service (or rural sociology), and (e) more adequate libraries (including the best library of Georgia history and literature in the country).

THE FIRST WORKS REPORT

The reorganization of higher education in Georgia was significantly influenced by the survey committee report written by George A. Works and submitted in 1933. Among the recommendations *not* followed by the Regents, however, were several concerning the composition of the Board. The membership of the Board of Regents, according to the survey committee, should consist of ten or twelve members appointed to longer terms (either ten or twelve years) and should not include the Governor as an *ex officio* member. Regents appointed to the Board should represent the State's economic and cultural interests but *not* its congressional districts. The reasoning of the consultants was explicit: the chief executives should not appoint a majority of the Regents or exercise undue influence. Citing the National Association of State Universities, the survey committee pointed out that "the theory (of *ex officio* membership) is thoroughly unsound, the practice is even worse."

The Regents did follow (eventually) the recommendation that the chancellor, and *not* the chairman of the Board, should be the chief executive officer. They were more reluctant, however, in appointing an executive secretary "properly trained in educational and statistical techniques, [and] charged . . . with the necessary duty of assembling, analyzing, and interpreting the regular and special reports of the operations of the several branches of the University System" (1933 *Annual Report*).

Also followed was the recommendation that "responsibility for work at the high school level" be placed on local school authorities. Ignored was a similar recommendation that the "local character of the junior college and the functions which it has in the program of education point to the desirability of the transfer of the junior college to local communities" (p. 29). Referring to a commission report in California, the survey committee acknowledged a national trend for junior colleges as "the last stage of the upper or secondary school period of common schooling" and stated that as junior colleges became an integral part of secondary education, they should be placed under the State Board of Education.

Although the 1933 survey report recommended the reduction of the University System of Georgia to no more than nine or ten units, the composition of the System became six senior institutions, six junior colleges, three historically black institutions, and two experiment stations. Yielding to local pressures, the Regents resorted to such actions as closing Georgia State College for Men in Tifton (a four-year institution) but opening Abraham Baldwin Agricultural College (a two-year college). In similar manner, the Regents transferred General University Extension from the University of Georgia and the Evening School of Commerce from Georgia Tech to an independent unit that became the University System of Georgia Center.

THE SECOND WORKS REPORT

In 1940 the Board of Regents again obtained funds from the General Education Board for "a re-study" of conditions in the University System. Dr. George A. Works was employed as director of the survey and his report, delayed until 1943, gives an overview of higher education in Georgia on the eve of World War II. Drawing heavily from his earlier report, Works documented the limited support given public higher education in the depression years and defined the problems and issues that would confront the University System when the national emergency was over.

The limited support given public higher education was shown by a record of ten consecutive years in which the state funds received by the University System fell short of the funds appropriated by the General Assembly. Not until 1940 did the University System receive its full state appropriation of $1.75 million. Failure to implement the recommendations of the earlier Works Report was shown by repeated recommendations: (a) to strengthen the Chancellor's professional staff through the appointment of a vice chancellor responsible for fiscal and budgetary matters; (b) to adopt uniform budgetary forms and procedures for the separate units and a complete, consolidated budget for the University System; (c) to separate purchasing for the University System from the office of the state purchasing agent; and (d) to develop a more serviceable committee structure to assist the Chancellor in his systemwide administrative duties.

In reviewing the status and support of the three state-supported colleges for blacks, Works reaffirmed the earlier recommendation that "a more liberal policy of support" was needed. The need for better support was shown by the low faculty salaries in the black colleges—and the survey committee asked that "more ample state support" be put as "the first and most important recommendation of this section" of their report. Significantly, the second Works Report recommended: (a) the material strengthening of undergraduate, general education programs at the three institutions; (b) the strengthening of professional training in agriculture, home economics, and teacher education; and (c) the provision of scholarships for graduate and professional study. Within these recommendations the report noted that Atlanta University "is in a position to meet the needs of students in certain fields of graduate and professional study" and asked the Chancellor, along with the three presidents of the black institutions, to prepare a list of such institutions acceptable to the Board of Regents.

In the area of student services, the Works Report suggested that progress had been made—but again, significant progress had not been made. To meet such lack of progress, the survey staff recommended the appointment of "a coordinator of student personnel services" but hastened to add that "an Assistant to the Chancellor and a Business Manager" should be given precedence. Noting that the University System had appointed a University Examiner to develop "through tests and measurements a competent program of student personnel and guidance" (p. 92), the survey staff endorsed the need for "inquiry and experimentation" in student personnel work and specifically pointed out the importance of diagnosing reading disabilities, poor study habits, and other learning difficulties that students may have had. Further recommendations included: (a) the development of a statewide testing program in the high school, (b) a special study of student financial aid, (c) the "cooperative interpretation" of the University System through better publicity and conferences of high school principals and counselors, (d) better housing for students, (e) and a uniform system of application blanks, student record forms, etc.

Graduate education and research were treated in the second Works Report in a chapter entitled "Miscellaneous Problems." Graduate instruction was offered exclusively at the University of Georgia and Georgia Tech. Discussed at greater length in the same chapter were the problems of the University System of Georgia Center, the only unit of the University System not accredited by the Southern Association of Colleges and Schools. Among the problems discussed by the Works Survey Committee were: (a) the dubious offering of three years of coursework in the liberal arts at the Center, (b) the heavy reliance on part-time instructors drawn from the business community, (c) excessive teaching loads, and (d) the institution's sole dependence on student fees for income.

The concluding chapter of the second Works Report dealt with the finances of the University System and depicted in detail the financial support given public higher education in Georgia. Virtually all data were for 1940-41, the last year of operations before the nation's entry into World War II.

The figures told a discouraging story. With a per capita income of $297, Georgians could look only to Mississippians, Arkansans, Alabamians, and South Carolinians as making less. Yet, Georgians spent only 39 cents each on higher education while their sister states spent at least 53 cents (Mississippi) and as much as 84 cents (Alabama). As the largest unit of the University System, the University of Georgia enrolled the full-time equivalent of 3,901 students but had only $1.08 million to spend on their education. West Georgia, the smallest unit, had only $70,582 to spend.

The cost per student-credit-hour in the University System ranged from $6.15 at the University to $2.25 at the University System Center. From the University's per-student-credit-hour cost, 49 cents was spent on administration and general overhead; $1.13 was spent on plant operation and maintenance; 43 cents was spent on the library; leaving $4.10 for instruction. Each of the junior colleges spent less than $2.00 per student-credit-hour.

Full-time-student expenditures ranged from $277 at UGA to $101 at the University System Center. Only the University, Georgia Teachers, and Georgia State Woman's College in Valdosta, among the senior institutions, spent as much as $10 per student for books. Within the University of Georgia, instructional costs ranged from $17.50 per student-credit-hour in education to $2.28 in journalism.

The survey staff strove to demonstrate the merits of unit costs in financing and budgeting. They recommended that each institution submit its annual budget to the Regents in terms of unit costs, using the full-time-student equivalent as the basis. They made a particularly strong case for increased support by pointing out that the actual appropriation to higher education had decreased since the University System was created, having been reduced 40 percent in a single year (1938-1939). Appropriations were reduced despite an increase of 70 percent in student enrollment (from 8,035 students in 1933-1934 to 13,736 in 1940-1941).

The final recommendations made in the second Works Report called for increased salaries for administrators, faculty, and staff; increased support for graduate instruction; more liberal support for the Division of General Extension and the

University System of Georgia Center; "much more ample facilities . . . and provision for instruction" for the higher education of blacks; and the addition of $50,000 to funds for miscellaneous purposes. If granted, the suggested budgetary increases would come to $600,000 and have raised the University System's then current income to a total of $2.5 million.

RECURRENT THEMES AND ISSUES

The early years of the Board of Regents and the two Works reports are reviewed at length because: (1) they depict the difficulties of establishing a statewide system of public higher education under extremely adverse conditions, and (2) they identify many recurring problems, issues, and concerns in public higher education. Each of these problems, issues, and/or concerns were considered by later Boards and survey committees, and each was dealt with in terms of the conditions and situations prevailing at the time.

Recurring educational issues were found in: (1) agriculture, (2) engineering, (3) business, (4) teacher education, (5) minority access, and (6) general education. Organizational and governance problems were found in: (7) the geographical distribution of institutions and programs, (8) financing and funding, (9) student services, (10) the mission of two-year colleges, (11) programs for part-time, adult students, and (12) the training of physicians and nurses. Each of these issues or problems had a direct bearing on the quality of postsecondary education and on the public's changing expectations for education beyond the high school.

> *Agriculture*: Both Works reports noted the University System's need to integrate resident instruction, extension services, and applied research in agriculture. The need for integration of these functions was identified as the most important issue faced by the Board of Regents in the field of agriculture. As for veterinary medicine, it was recommended that its professional curriculum at the University

of Georgia be discontinued. This recommendation for such unification was eventually resolved in 1951, but the nature and extent of agricultural programs continued to be a recurrent theme.

Engineering: In 1940 the most pressing problem in engineering education was the inadequacy of its funding. Georgia Tech's annual expenditures were barely one million dollars and the per-student instructional cost of $270 was regarded by experts as "wholly inadequate." The institution's role as something more than a local or state institution was noted, and the State's failure to provide adequate facilities was deemed contrary to the State's desire to exercise control. Specifically noted in the second Works Report was the question of presidential longevity and replacement by someone "widely recognized for his standing in science or engineering as well as for his qualification as an administrator and leader" (p. 76).

Business: The Board of Regents' reasons for closing Georgia Tech's School of Commerce and transferring its Evening School to an independent Department of Adult Education were: (1) the State could not afford two competing schools of commerce, and (2) strong schools of commerce could not be developed independently of "high-grade work in economics, history, and government" (p. 11). The Regents thought it advisable to develop "a real center of adult education in Atlanta" by transferring the University of Georgia's Department of General University Extension to Atlanta to work in conjunction with the newly formed Evening School of Commerce. Similar reasoning would be used in later years in the establishment of Georgia State University.

Teacher Education: The preparation of public school teachers as a responsibility of institutions of higher education and the difficulties of cooperation among accrediting agencies, schools of education, state boards of education, and governing boards were an obvious *and* pressing issue. By 1943 the University System was "well equipped with buildings and equipment" to train teachers for public schools, but adequate funds were not yet available "to hold or to attract the type of teachers needed in our university system and our public school system" (1944 *Annual Report*).

Minority Access: In his 1943-1944 annual report, Chancellor Sanford did not address the recommendations of the second Works Report concerning the status and support of the State's historically black institutions. In the midst of World War II, he discussed the difficulties and benefits of specialized training programs for military personnel, the decreases in civilian students, and the prospects of the GI Bill and other changes on postwar education.

General Education: The influence of World War II on higher education was seen in the mobilization of college campuses to assist in the war effort. Chancellor Sanford, in 1944, was convinced that "technical education on the college level will have a permanent, and not a subsidiary place in the educational program" (p. 47). Neither the nation nor the community could afford the "tragedy of undeveloped talent."

Geographical Distribution: Despite war-time restrictions, the excessive duplication of programs and courses was a matter of concern in 1943-1944. The University of Georgia, according to its president, offered too many courses and the faculty was urged to study curricular offerings and to eliminate courses of dubious value. Chancellor Sanford rejected the "ancient idol" that the best colleges were those that offered "the greatest number of subjects or the greatest variety of courses" (p. 38).

Financing and Funding: Student *per capita* expenditures at the University of Georgia were $116, the lowest among state universities of the region. At Georgia Tech, *per capita* expenditures were $90, as compared to $148 at North Carolina

State, $100 at Auburn, and $227 at Louisiana Tech. Cost comparisons for teachers colleges and colleges for women told the same story and prompted Chairman Marion Smith of the Board of Regents to ask if the State of Georgia could afford to do less than the average of other southeastern states?

Student Services: The second Works Report devoted an entire chapter to student personnel services in the University System. There was an urgent need to correct substandard conditions in residence halls and to adjust dormitory fees to the quality of facilities and services. Better provisions were to be made for the coordination of personnel services, health services were to be improved and extended, and the importance of diagnostic services for special student problems was to be recognized. Among the recommendations were a statewide testing program in the high schools, workshops for personnel officers, and a uniform system of student records-keeping.

Two-Year Colleges: In studying the State's junior colleges, the second Works Report turned up numerous problems. There were difficulties in reconciling two years of general education with advanced or specialized training, such as engineering, and a five-year program for junior college transfers might be the preferred solution. Chancellor Sanford, in his annual report, was convinced that at least two junior colleges should be changed into engineering schools that would prepare students to enter the senior division of Georgia Tech or any other similar technological institution.

Adult Education: The 1943 survey staff found many problems at the University System of Georgia Center. No useful educational purpose was served by offering three years of liberal arts, and resources at the Center were not concentrated sufficiently on strong programs in business. The Center was too dependent on part-time instructors, student fees, and excessive teaching loads for its programs and services.

The Center was also the only unit of the University System that was not accredited by the Southern Association of Colleges and Schools.

Physicians and Nurses: To help meet "a crying demand for physicians and nurses in Georgia," the Regents authorized in September 1944 a department of nursing at the Medical College. In a five-year nursing program, students could take their first two years at the University of Georgia, their next two years in Augusta or another approved hospital, and return to Athens for their fifth year. In a graduate nurses program, students could be given one year's academic credit for their training in a hospital school of nursing and earn a Bachelor of Science degree in nursing (or nursing education) through three additional years of work at the University of Georgia. Related to the training of physicians and nurses was the organization of public health districts, as opposed to county health departments that existed in only half of Georgia's 159 counties.

In reviewing the early years of the new University System, the accomplishments of the first decade must be regarded as commendable progress under adverse conditions. The reorganization of 26 separate and competitive state institutions and agencies into a centrally coordinated statewide system was not yet complete, but progressive steps had been taken toward educational respectability in the State's colleges and universities. The organization of the Board of Regents and the leadership of the Regents was an explicit acknowledgement of the State's responsibility for education beyond the high school and a public commitment to educational advancement.

Despite a national depression and shameful financial support, the Board of Regents was able to reduce its responsibility for secondary schoolwork by eliminating or upgrading the district A&M schools. By merging the three state institutions located in Athens, the Regents laid the foundation for a more comprehensive and viable state university. And by taking advantage of federal programs of assistance, various additions and improvements were made in the physical facilities of the University System.

Until wartime drafts and enlistments took their share of students, the total enrollment in the State's colleges had more than doubled. In 1930 no more than 6,000 students could be counted by the University of Georgia and its branches. By 1940 the total enrollment had reached 13,736 students (an increase of at least 129%). In comparison to the estimated enrollment in 1930, the enrollment of 8,035 students in 1933 makes the new University System look even better. Less than three out of every 1,000 Georgians were students in a state-supported college, but reorganization of the University System had given better credibility to the State's efforts to provide a college education to Georgians who could afford it.

Although in great need of better financial and moral support, an organizational structure for public higher education was in place and commitments to a three-tier system of universities, senior colleges, and junior colleges were evident. Organizational problems persisted in many areas, such as the Regents' efforts to upgrade the three public colleges for blacks. Not until 1939 had the Regents been able to close the State Teachers' and Agricultural College at Forsyth and to consolidate its meager resources with the Fort Valley High and Industrial School. Even then, the establishment of Fort Valley State College was possible only with the assistance of the Rosenwald Fund. The mission and role of the public historically black institutions, as an integral part of public higher education, would not become a major item on the Regents' agenda until the 1960s.

Efforts to cope with organizational, administrative, funding, political, and social problems left many unresolved issues in educational programs and services. Significant progress had been made in attracting more competent faculty members to units of the University System but political appointees in academic positions were still detrimental to the overall improvement of higher education. Commendable steps were taken in inter-collegiate coordination by requiring survey courses and common examinations, but with continued growth, coordination would prove difficult to manage. All such problems aside, World War II brought signs of economic recovery and gave an additional boost to the University System's growth and its efforts to gain educational respectability.

CHAPTER TWO
Status and Authority: 1941-1945

> *Such matters are altogether in the control of the Board of*
> *Regents, provided the Board follows its own established*
> *rules and regulations. . . . It was the fact that we did not*
> *follow such established and agreed-upon procedures that*
> *has caused our troubles.*
>
> Chairman Sandy Beavers, *1941 Annual Report*

The Board of Regents, with various modifications such as an increase in membership and inclusion of the Governor as an *ex officio* member, operated under statutory authority from its inception in 1932 until August 3, 1943. At that time the citizens of Georgia ratified a constitutional amendment establishing the Board of Regents of the University System of Georgia as a constitutional body. Two years later the ratified amendment was incorporated into the State Constitution of 1945. The membership of the Board was increased to fifteen, one each from the ten congressional districts and five from the state at large. The Governor was excluded as an *ex officio* member.

The events leading to the Board of Regents' constitutional status were the University System's severest challenge and the means by which constitutional status was granted is (a half-century later) the general public's strongest endorsement. The conditions under which several administrative officials were dismissed led to an investigation by the Southern Association of Colleges and Schools and subsequent dis-accreditation of ten University System institutions holding membership in the Association. The institutions affected by the Southern Association's action were: (1) the University of Georgia, (2) Georgia School of Technology, (3) Georgia State College for Women, (4) Georgia State Woman's College, (5) Georgia Teachers College, (6) Georgia Southwestern, (7) Middle Georgia, (8) North Georgia, (9) South Georgia, and (10) West Georgia. The three public colleges for blacks were not involved in the action because the Southern Association did not at that time accredit the historically black institutions in its region.

In November 1941 the investigating committee held a hearing in Atlanta and invited all members of the Board of Regents and all presidents of institutions belonging to the Association. Present at the meeting were representatives of the Council on Medical Education, the American Association of Schools of Law, the American Bar Association, the American Association of Teachers Colleges, and Phi Beta Kappa Honor Society. Participants in the hearing included a committee from the Board of Regents, alumni and student committees from Georgia Tech and the University of Georgia, and the presidents of institutions affected by the recommendations of the investigating committee. Also participating were other educational officials such as the superintendent of Atlanta Public Schools (Willis A. Sutton), the president of Emory University (Goodrich C. White), and the president of Agnes Scott (J.R. McCain). Serving on the investigating committee were the presidents of Vanderbilt (O.C. Carmichael, chairman), Sewanee (Alexander Guerry), and Florida (John J. Tigert) universities.

In December 1941 the committee issued a report in which it concluded that the University System of Georgia had been the victim of "unprecedented and unjustifiable political interference." The Governor of Georgia had violated not only "sound educational policy, but proper democratic procedure in insisting upon the resignation of members of the Board of Regents to appoint to that body men who would do his bidding." The Board of Regents had violated sound educational procedure "in dismissals and appointment of staff members." The committee further concluded that "every institution in the System is affected by the precedents established and by the actions already taken." Where such conditions exist, the committee stated, "there can be no effective educational program."

The specific findings of the committee were particularly detrimental to the purposes and functions of the University

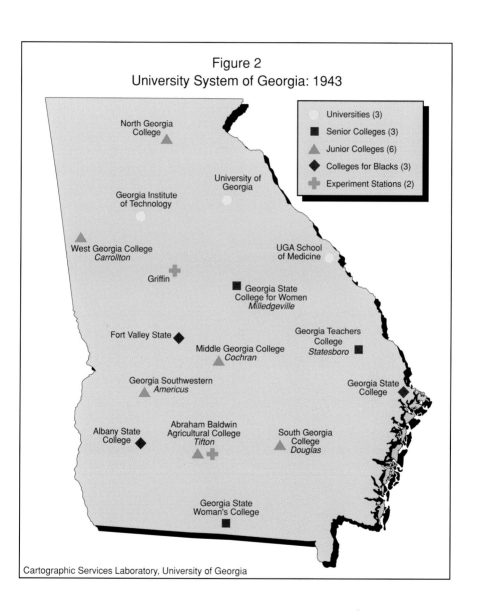

Figure 2
University System of Georgia: 1943

Universities (3)
Senior Colleges (3)
Junior Colleges (6)
Colleges for Blacks (3)
Experiment Stations (2)

North Georgia College

University of Georgia

Georgia Institute of Technology

West Georgia College
Carrollton

UGA School of Medicine

Griffin

Georgia State College for Women
Milledgeville

Fort Valley State

Georgia Teachers College
Statesboro

Middle Georgia College
Cochran

Georgia Southwestern
Americus

Georgia State College

Albany State College

Abraham Baldwin Agricultural College
Tifton

South Georgia College
Douglas

Georgia State Woman's College

Cartographic Services Laboratory, University of Georgia

System. Finding that Governor Eugene Talmadge had first requested that the Board of Regents dismiss Dr. Walter D. Cocking, dean of education at the University of Georgia, and then denounced the Regents' action when they failed to do so, the committee detailed the Governor's subsequent actions in: (1) forcing the resignation of three members of the Board, (2) appointing three members who would do his bidding, (3) notifying Dean Cocking that he would be tried again, and (4) summoning President Marvin Pittman of Georgia Teachers College for trial on the same date.

From the record the committee noted that Dean Cocking and President Pittman were dismissed "by the same vote" and with the same "mockery of democratic procedure." The committee was convinced by its examination of the evidence that the charges against the two were "either spurious or entirely unsupported by the evidence."

The committee also found that in addition to Dean Cocking and President Pittman, the Board of Regents had dismissed— without hearings, adequate reasons, or due notice—Dr. J. Curtis Dixon, vice chancellor of the University System; Dr. Charles M. Destler, chairman of the Division of Social Science at Georgia Teachers College; the dean of women and another faculty member at Georgia Teachers College; one faculty member at North Georgia College; and three staff members of the Department of Agricultural Extension.

In a related matter the committee found that the position of dean of men had been filled at the Georgia School of Technology without the recommendation of either President Brittain or Chancellor Sanford. The committee recognized that the appointee did not accept the position but that fact did not alter the conviction of the committee that the Board of Regents had violated sound educational policy in the appointment. The committee also recognized that the Governor under the statutes of the State had the authority to modify the University System's budget in any way he saw fit. He had the authority to delete or modify any item of expenditure or remove any individual from the payroll without the Board's approval. To the committee, however, "arbitrary power of this kind in the hands of any individual or agency is a threat to sound procedure in the operation of an educational system."

The committee made but two recommendations: (1) that the ten (named) institutions be dropped from membership in the Southern Association of Colleges and Schools, and (2) that the suspension take effect September 1, 1942 and continue until removed by vote at the Association's next (or later) annual meeting. The committee's recommendations were judicious in not taking immediate effect and challenging in view of the forthcoming gubernatorial election to be held in the fall of 1942. The date of the committee's report was December 3rd, just four days prior to the United States entry into the Second World War.

The decisiveness of the 1942 gubernatorial election was further testimony to the damaging effects of political interference. The incumbent Governor was defeated by a candidate committed to the University System's re-accreditation. The successful candidate received 58 percent of the popular vote and 64 percent of the county unit vote that were then required in Georgia primaries. Upon taking office on January 12, 1943 Governor Ellis Arnall (1943-1947) gained legislative cooperation in submitting a constitutional amendment that would grant constitutional authority to the Board of Regents. The House and Senate bills for the constitutional amendment were passed without a dissenting vote within eleven days of the new Governor's oath of office. Upon passage of the House and Senate bills, the Governor (by executive order) appointed a new Board of Regents, reinstating several members who had resigned under partisan political pressure. The constitutional amendment was ratified by Georgia voters on August 3, 1943 and became a section in the Constitution of 1877. Although the issue was convincingly resolved by the Georgia electorate, the process had taken more than two years and the total cost in public and human resources was incalculable.

THE CONSTITUTION OF 1945

In March 1943 the General Assembly passed a resolution providing for a commission to revise the State's Constitution. The commission, consisting of 26 members and led by Governor Arnall, submitted its revision to the General Assembly in January 1945, and on August 7, 1945 the new Constitution was approved by the voters of the State. Over 90 percent of its provisions were drawn from the amended Constitution of 1877.

The constitutional authority of the Board of Regents was unaltered. Article VIII, Section IV provided for "the government, control, and management" of the University System and "all of its institutions" by a fifteen-member Board that was representative of the ten congressional Districts and the state at large. Appointments to the Board were for terms of seven years each, a stipulation related to the governor's four-year term of office. At that time the governor could succeed himself, and the staggered seven-year appointments of Regents would thereby prevent a single governor from appointing all members of the Board. In the event of vacancies caused by resignation, death, or from causes other than the expiration of term, the Board of Regents was authorized (in a provision later altered) to elect a successor who would hold office until the end of the next session of the General Assembly.

Strongly implied in the conditions of appointment were the independence of the Board of Regents as a governing body, and its freedom from political interference by the governor and the state legislature. Also implicit was the Regents' authority and independence in electing a chancellor who would recommend institutional presidents to the Board. In turn, institutional presidents would recommend to the Chancellor the faculty and staff appointments for their particular units. Directly related to powers of appointment were the Regents' authority and responsibility in all matters pertaining to the dismissal of faculty members.

In brief, the new Constitution gave the Board of Regents broad governing powers for its own procedures, the internal operations of the Chancellor's staff, and the administration, management, and/or control of the respective units of the University System. Not only was the Board responsible for system-wide policies, the Board was responsible for institutional policies affecting daily operations on the various campuses. The gist of the Regents' constitutional status was their authority and responsibility as a state-level governing board for all public institutions of higher education regarded as units of the University System of Georgia.

POWERS AND POLICIES OF THE REGENTS

The Board of Regents executes its constitutional responsibilities in two primary ways: (a) by adopting policies to provide general guidelines for governing the University System, and (b) by electing the Chancellor of the System and, upon his recommendation, presidents of the institutions who are given the responsibility and the authority for the administration of the System in accord with the adopted policies (*Policy Manual*, Board of Regents [2nd ed.], 1982). In the execution of its responsibilities, the Board of Regents has the power to make "such reasonable rules and regulations as are necessary for the performance of its duties." The Regents' powers of appointment cover "professors, educators, stewards, or any other officers necessary for all of the schools in the University System," the discontinuance of their services when required for "the good of the System or any of its schools or institutions," and the determination of their salaries and/or compensations. All such actions are taken in accordance with state law and must not be in conflict with the State Constitution or the authority granted other Constitutional agencies.

In implementing their broad powers as a statewide governing board, the Regents have been primarily concerned with institutions, programs, and personnel. In the early years of their new powers the Regents were responsible for six senior institutions, seven junior colleges, three colleges for blacks, and three experiment stations. Also included among the Regents' governing responsibilities was the Department of Adult Education with its two divisions, the Georgia Evening College and the Division of General Extension in Atlanta. The officers of the first constitutional Board were Chairman Marion Smith, Vice-Chairman Sandy Beaver, Chancellor S.V. Sanford, Secretary L.R. Siebert, and Treasurer W. Wilson Noyes. The standing committees on which members of the Board served were the committees on education, finance, organization and law, agriculture, and visitation.

The Board's concern with programs at that time was directed to the postwar years, the enrichment or modification of coursework for returning servicemen, and efforts to strengthen the State's teacher education programs. New curricula were nec-- essary in the postwar era to accommodate changes in "the concept of the place of women in society" and to prepare students for occupations in the fields of management and health care. In later years the committee structure of the Board and the Chancellor's staff changed with demands for new institutions and with the many changes in personnel and public expectations.

MEMBERS OF THE BOARD

Neither state law nor Regents policies specify qualifications for individual members of the Board. Each Regent need only be appointed by the governor and confirmed by the Senate. Public expectations are explicit, however, and members of the Board serve in the public interest and not at the pleasure of the governor. In the public's estimation, appointment to the Board of Regents is the highest honor that the State of Georgia can confer upon nonelected officials.

Since the Board's creation one hundred and thirty-nine citizens of Georgia have served as members. At least twenty-seven Regents have been re-appointed for one or more terms and one Regent (Carey Williams) served for thirty years. Almost without exception, the individual Regents have been leaders in agriculture, business, finance, real estate, and the professions of law or medicine. Until the 1970s most Regents had been male, white, financially secure, college-educated, and Protestant. Many have been graduates of the institutions for which they were constitutionally responsible.

In keeping with other members of governing boards, Regents regard their major responsibilities as the review and approval of institutional policy decisions, the appointment of presidents, and the approval of other decisions related to faculties and students. As members of a statewide governing board, Regents are also responsible for the allocation (among institutions) of public funds and resources. Members of the Board of Regents may also serve as trustees of private or independent colleges (Best, 1988).

OFFICERS OF THE BOARD

The administrative structure and activities of the central offices have changed as the Board of Regents and University System institutions have acquired new functions and responsibilities. The duties and responsibilities of the officers were later defined in the following manner:

> The *Chairman* presides at meetings of the Board with the authority to vote, appoints members of all committees, and designates the chairman of each committee. He or she is an *ex officio* member of all committees with the authority to vote. Upon the authority of the Board (and in the name of Board of Regents) the chairman executes all notes, bonds, deeds, contracts, and other documents requiring the seal of the Board of Regents of the University System of Georgia. The chairman also submits the annual report of the Board of Regents to the governor (Bylaws, Article IV, Section 5). The power and influence of the chairman has varied over the years and with the capabilities of individuals serving in the position. In the early years of the University System the chairman served somewhat as a chief executive officer while the chancellor served primarily as a chief of staff. This arrangement was no longer necessary when Phillip Weltner, a member of the Board, became chancellor. Later chairmen of

the Board have provided leadership as the strengths and weaknesses of chancellors required.

The *Vice Chairman* performs the duties and has the powers of the chairman during the latter's absence or disability (Bylaws, Article IV, Section 6). As the chairmanship became a rotating position in the 1980s, vice chairmen were elected with expectations of being the next chairman.

The *Chancellor* is elected by the Regents and holds office at the pleasure of the Board. In the event of a vacancy in the chancellorship, the Board names an acting chancellor who serves until the office of the chancellor is filled. The chancellor is now clearly identified as the chief administrative officer of the University System *and* the chief executive officer of the Board of Regents. He is responsible to the Board for the prompt and effective execution of all resolutions, policies, rules, and regulations adopted by the Board for the operation of the entire University System and for the government of any and all of its institutions. With such responsibilities comes broad discretionary powers that enable him to perform all duties prescribed by the Board (BR Minutes, 1980-81, p. 241). Since 1932 eight individuals have served as chancellor with two others serving as acting chancellor (without later appointment as chancellor). The nature of the leadership provided by each has necessarily varied with the individual's understanding of his responsibilities and the different challenges to which the chief administrative officer of a statewide university system must respond.

The *Executive Vice Chancellor* is elected by the Board upon recommendation of the chancellor. The executive vice chancellor acts as the chancellor's deputy and speaks for the chancellor (in his absence). All members of the chancellor's staff report to the executive vice chancellor who is responsible for organizing the work of the staff and for its oversight.

The executive vice chancellor also reviews all appointments and budget amendments in the University System. He arranges for the preparation of budgets, building programs, and the agenda for meetings of the Board of Regents. As the chancellor's deputy the executive vice chancellor also conducts day-to-day institutional operations that do not interfere with the presidents' direct and immediate access to the chancellor (BR Minutes, 1970-71, pp. 24-25).

The *Executive Secretary* is also elected by the Board upon the recommendation of the chancellor. He is required to be present at all meetings of the Board and at committee meetings except as otherwise determined by the Board. He keeps an accurate record of the proceedings of the meetings of the Board and of committees and is responsible for maintaining the Policy Manual. He receives and processes all applications for reviews and other appeals submitted to the Board. In addition, the executive secretary keeps in safe custody the seal of the Board and affixes the seal to those documents requiring it. He is the custodian of all deeds and evidence of title to the tangible property of the University System, acts as general counsel for the Board, advises and consults with the Chancellor and the several institutions on all legal matters, and serves as the principal liaison between the Board and the Attorney-General's office (By-laws, Article IV, Section 8).

The *Treasurer* is another Officer of the Board elected by the Board upon the recommendation of the Chancellor. He is present at all meetings of the Board except as otherwise determined by the Board. In the performance of his duties he is placed under bond in an amount determined by the Board (BR Minutes, 1980-81, p. 241).

THE CHANCELLOR'S STAFF

As the chancellor's duties and responsibilities have expanded with the growth of the University System, his staff was enlarged accordingly. The position of assistant chancellor was used in the 1950s and a director of plant operations was added to the chancellor's staff in the 1960s. The title of vice chancellor was not used until 1964 when Dr. S. Walter Martin became vice chancellor for academic affairs prior to becoming acting chancellor. In 1966 Dr. Fred C. Davison became vice chancellor and Dr. Mario J. Goglia became vice chancellor-research. Two new vice chancellors were added the following year when a vice chancellor-services was appointed and the position of treasurer became that of vice chancellor-fiscal affairs and treasurer. In such ways positions on the chancellor's staff were given functional titles and a functional division of staff responsibilities has continued since that time. The position of vice chancellor is now used for the administrative functions of student services, research and planning, and information technology. Positions of assistant vice chancellor are used in the areas of academic affairs, affirmative action, facilities, fiscal affairs, planning, and research while an assistant-to-the-chancellor title is used in public relations and information services.

PROCEDURAL POLICIES

The Board of Regents, under its bylaws, meets monthly on the second Wednesday. Special meetings may be called by the chairman upon written request to the executive secretary, or by the executive secretary upon written requests from four or more members of the Board. All meetings are held in the Board Room of the Regents unless otherwise determined by the Board. Meetings begin at 10:00 a.m. with eight members of the Board constituting a quorum. Parliamentary rules of the State Senate are followed in conducting the business of the Board.

Standing Committees of the Board are: (1) Executive Committee, consisting of the chairman, the immediate past chairman, the vice chairman, and the chancellor *ex officio* non-voting; (2) Committee on Buildings and Grounds; (3) Committee on Desegregation; (4) Committee on Education; (5) Committee on Finance and Business; (6) Committee on Health Professions;

(7) Committee on Organization and Law; (8) Committee on Research and Extension; and (9) Committee on Visitation. Each standing committee consists of not less than three, nor more than five members (*Policy Manual*, 1982).

Academic and administrative policies for the institutions of the University System are developed through an Advisory Council of institutional presidents and two non-voting members from each institution who are selected by their respective presidents. Under the Advisory Council are various academic committees, representing the programs of instruction within each of the units, and various administrative committees, addressing such matters as personnel, student financial aid, and general extension. The academic and administrative committees make recommendations to the Advisory Council which, in turn, makes recommendations to the chancellor.

THE CONSTITUTION OF 1982

In 1982 a new State Constitution was adopted in which two slight modifications were made in the Board of Regents' authority. The Regents themselves can no longer appoint a temporary successor in the event of a vacancy on the Board; that privilege was reserved for the governor. Another slight difference between the 1982 Constitution and the 1945 Constitution pertains to "approval by majority vote in the House of Representatives and the Senate" of new public colleges, junior colleges, and universities created in the Board's exercise of its "exclusive authority" to create such institutions. Approval by the General Assembly was *not* required in Board decisions to change the status of any institution existing prior to the 1982 Constitution.

The Constitution of 1982, as shown in Appendix A, sustains and enhances the Board of Regents authority and responsibility for the State's comprehensive system of public higher education. As a constitutional board, the Regents have extensive powers for the governance and administration of 34 public institutions and for the implementation of public and institutional policy.

In all matters dealing with state and federal government, the Regents serve as the representatives of public higher education within the State. In the coalescence of its governing authority under a single constitutional board, the Regents also serve as a safeguard against political interference and/or undue public or private intervention. In meeting their responsibilities the Regents also serve as a public advocate of higher education as essential to the State's social, economic, technological, and cultural advancement.

Careful review would show that the Board of Regents uses its authority sparingly. Commendable restraint is evident in the setting of both system and institutional policies. The purposes of the System itself have always been stated in general terms with a minimum of educational doctrine. Institutions have been defined mostly by level and major functions instead of specific missions or roles. Programs have been classified in broad terms that suggest areas of teaching and learning and not in terms of state needs and public expectations.

The administrative structure and functions of the central offices were, and would continue to be, a matter of cut-and-try. As different individuals were appointed to administrative positions, duties and responsibilities were defined to fit personal qualifications and position requirements. When the demands of the position were incompatible with the capabilities of the person, the position was reorganized or abolished in search of a more suitable fit. The chancellor's position as chief academic officer of the institutions and as chief executive officer for the Board, along with the positions of executive secretary and treasurer, have been the constants in central administration. Other administrative and staff functions have varied appreciably with the times and the conditions imposed.

The authority and responsibility of the chancellor are crucial to the effective administration and governance of the University System—just as the authority and responsibility of presidents are essential to institutional leadership. No other appointed or elected public official demonstrates more clearly the state's need for educational leadership or serves so well as a spokesman for public policy in higher education. And with the possible exception of the governor, no other public official experiences the public respect shown the University System chancellor.

If two guiding principles may be identified for the policy decisions of the Board (and the State's purpose in providing public resources), one can be called self-sufficiency and the other geographical accessibility. The first principle was evident in the early years as Georgians accepted responsibility for their own education and lessened their dependence on other states and institutions for educated, professionally prepared participants in the State's economic and cultural life. The second principle became increasingly evident in the postwar years when higher education became the focal point of "rising expectations." Geographical accessibility was evident in the location of institutions inherited by the Regents and geographical distribution became a dominant factor in the establishment of later institutions.

CHAPTER THREE
Expansion and Improvement: 1946-1960

> *In spending money for the expansion and improvement of the institutions of the System, it is essential that the expenditures be made for the attainment of clearly defined institutional objectives and that they be made in accordance with a well formulated, long-range plan of development.*
> Chancellor Harmon W. Caldwell, *1951 Annual Report*

The first fourteen years (1932-1946) of the University System are appreciated best as years in which the Regents reorganized the State's institutions of public higher education and established their authority as a statewide governing board. No institution, however, deserved status as a full-fledged university and despite surveys by outside educators, the University System was not yet a statewide system of colleges and universities serving the educational needs of Georgia residents. Georgians, like other southerners, were dependent upon other states for much of their scientific, professional, and technical expertise. The years 1946-1960 can be viewed as years of postwar growth and expansion, as years in which progress was more rapid and more substantive.

THE STRAYER REPORT

In 1949 the Board of Regents again found funds for a statewide survey by out-of-state experts and specialists. The survey began in September of that year and was concluded on December 15th in time for consideration and action by the General Assembly convening in January 1950. The director of the survey was George D. Strayer, formerly director of the Division of Field Studies at Teachers College, Columbia University. Although submitted as "a staff report," the published report has always been known as the "Strayer Report." Like its predecessors, the Works reports, the Strayer Report was simply entitled "A Report of a Survey of the University System of Georgia."

More extensive in scope and more intensive in its analyses than the Works reports, the Strayer Report was a comprehensive study of the University System of Georgia in the years following World War II and the closest thing to a plan for systemwide development the Regents had until the Governor's (Carl Sanders) Commission To Improve Education in the 1960s. The Strayer Report addressed each of the issues identified in the second Works report and arrived at many recommendations that were compatible with the earlier surveys but made some recommendations that were contrary.

The Strayer Report began by meeting head-on one of the University System's most irritating problems. The first lines in the report read, "The competitive ambitions of individual institutions must be subordinated to the responsibilities of the statewide system of higher education" (p. 1). The report then restated the Regents' responsibilities, their delegation of specific activities and functions to the separate institutions, and their maintenance of authority through "supervisory officers." To Strayer, the most important contribution that any institution could make to the social and economic development of the State was the preparation of professional personnel for service in the State's colleges and schools. Explicit recognition was given the University System's responsibility to prepare college and university teachers and administrators.

The report stressed that to prepare professionally trained teachers for the public schools, the University System should recognize a minimum standard of four years of college training and move from there to higher standards. Facilities were to be improved and increased for such purposes, with "a broad general education" as "a necessary portion of any program" (p. 11). Evidently to settle territorial squabbles, the survey staff recommended the form and level of programs that each institution should develop. Georgia Tech and the state's junior colleges were to enter no field of teacher education while the University of Georgia was to be the state's one comprehensive teacher preparatory institution. The "special fields" of education (agriculture, home economics, physical education, business education, fine and industrial arts) were "allocated" to the other institutions on the basis of faculties and facilities. Academic subjects (English, science, history, mathematics, etc.) were not similarly allocated but assumed to be a function of four-year colleges preparing high school teachers for specific fields.

In addition to laboratory schools for practice teaching, the University System needed programs for the inservice training of teachers already employed in the public schools. A need that could not "be too strongly emphasized" was in the areas of research, graduate work, and professional education. The University System's paucity of resources in these areas was charitably treated by the survey staff, but the discouraging state of public higher education was nonetheless evident. Recommended as "the one great center for graduate and professional education and for research" was the University of Georgia. The Georgia Institute of Technology was to be permitted to add a doctoral degree in mathematics to Ph.D.'s already authorized in physics and chemistry while the Medical College was to remain an independent unit and offer the master's degree in the clinical and technological fields of medicine.

Noting that in March 1949 the Regents had at last merged the Agricultural Experiment Stations and the Cooperative Extension Service with the UGA College of Agriculture, the survey staff endorsed the Regents' authority in matters of internal organization for the College of Agriculture and recommended the establishment of an agricultural research council. They then suggested that the organization and procedures of agricultural research might serve as a pattern for other organized research units within the University System.

The Strayer Report strongly emphasized the linkage of research with graduate education and endorsed the organization of graduate schools with a right to designate graduate faculty members who were qualified for graduate instruction. Such a school was also given the right to approve any course to be taken for graduate credit and have its own budgeted funds to encourage research and thereby tie research more firmly to graduate instruction.

In considering the diverse extension services offered within the University System, the survey staff concluded that an "institutional division" of extension services along geographical or functional lines was impractical and recommended the "voluntary or compulsory coordination" of extension services to form one statewide agency. Coordination was to be a responsibility of a system officer on the Chancellor's staff who would be assisted by an Extension Council representative of the various institutions. The general extension service of the University of Georgia had many elements which the survey staff believed applicable to the statewide effort.

Institutional Functions: The mission or role of each unit of the University System was well defined in the Strayer Report. Georgia Tech, the Medical College, North Georgia, Georgia State College for Women, and Georgia Teachers College were assigned distinctive missions in keeping with their titles and their historical development. Valdosta State was to be developed as a co-educational college of arts and sciences, with a program for preparing elementary school teachers. The University of Georgia, was to continue as the major institution in the University System with a full range of undergraduate, graduate, and professional programs and with broad applications of its research and extension services.

The delineation of roles for the historically black institutions was quite explicit. Fort Valley State was to be the State's college for emphasizing agriculture and home economics, with possibilities for granting master's degrees in those fields. Savannah State was to be developed in industrial and business fields, with secondary emphases on elementary teacher education and programs in the arts and sciences. Albany State was to be the State's college of arts and sciences, with a larger emphasis on elementary teacher education than the other two historically black institutions.

The difficult unit for the survey staff was the Atlanta Division of the University of Georgia. Although recommending independent status for the institution, the survey staff confined their recommendation to the awarding of bachelor's degrees in business administration. Only two years of academic work were to be given in arts and sciences but "pending the establishment of a junior college by the City of Atlanta," the institution was to continue offering two-year diploma programs in business. These recommendations were implemented six years later when the Atlanta Division became the Georgia State College of Business Administration.

In a separate chapter the Strayer Report fully delineated the role and functions of the State's junior colleges but recommended their disassociation from the University System. The junior college "movement" was depicted as the addition of upper division work to a state's common school system. Providing two-year vocational programs for students uninterested in a collegiate education, junior colleges nonetheless offered general education as a strong component of terminal or career curricula and served also to prepare students for transfer to four-year colleges, if they so desired. As "a local institution" a junior college also provided a program of adult education. Thus, they were to be administered by local school boards, or by another board representative of a larger area that was to constitute a junior college district. Junior colleges would be, of course, under the general supervision of the State Board of Education and the State was to continue to support them, along with funds raised through local taxation. Although eloquent in persuasion and fifteen pages in length, this particular chapter contained not one single recommendation ever implemented by the Board of Regents.

Postwar Adjustments: The Strayer Report was a milestone in the University System's development for many reasons. It depicted in great detail the status of public higher education in the years following World War II and demonstrated the changes in institutional composition that had taken place since the University System's creation seventeen years earlier. When the Strayer Report was received by the Regents, they were responsible for fifteen institutions of higher education, an appreciable reduction from the twenty-six units they had inherited. If the Evening School and Technical Institute of Georgia Tech were counted separately, the total number was seventeen. Three of these units remained colleges for blacks; five were two-year or junior colleges; and at least seven were senior institutions.

Only indirectly did the Strayer Report reveal the implementation or ignorance of recommendations found in the earlier Works reports. Middle Georgia and South Georgia colleges were still intact; North Georgia was a four-year college; and the Atlanta Division was accredited only by virtue of its designation as a division of the University of Georgia. Per-student instructional costs were still lower at the Atlanta Division ($195) than anywhere else and student fees still accounted for the majority of institutional income. Georgians still paid a higher proportion (34.2%) of their educational costs than other southerners (21.8%) or Americans (18.6%) did. And yet, the University System had grown significantly and was, by most measures, a stronger, more mature system of public higher education. Not unrelated to its growth and development was its weathering of disaccreditation by the Southern Association of Colleges and Schools in the early 1940s because of political interference and its later inclusion as a constitutional body in the new state Constitution adopted in 1945.

The Strayer Report may be read, nonetheless, as an indictment of educational quality following the unplanned growth of the postwar years. Returning veterans overcrowded classrooms as they took advantage of the G.I. Bill. Student housing, food services, and student personnel programs could only be judged as deplorable for most campuses. Dormitory facilities and services were frequently inadequate because of "deferred maintenance" during the war and their excessive use in the years immediately following. Overcrowding created, in many cases, what the survey staff regarded as "a serious health hazard" and the obsolescence of some buildings was "a grave menace" to student safety.

To solve its "deferred maintenance problems" the University System would need, according to survey staff estimates, almost $1.4 million—over $600,000 at Georgia Tech alone. With almost no exceptions, dormitories on the separate campuses were operated at an appreciable profit. Seldom had the need for planning been more clearly demonstrated.

Financing the Future: The Strayer Report gave close attention to the administration and governance of the University System; its budgeting, accounting, and reporting needs; and its organizational structure and procedures. The report then addressed the University System's need for adequate financing in its efforts to meet increased demands for education beyond the high school. Enrollments in the University System were shown as almost doubling (81.4%) in the decade of the 1940s and projected enrollments were given up to 1964-1965. Veterans were expected to have received all educational benefits by the mid-1950s, but the projected enrollments were necessarily low because of educational trends and developments that the survey staff could not take into consideration. The estimated demand for the services of the University System showed a decline until 1954-1955 and a slow, gradual increase until 1964-1965 when enrollments were expected to exceed 44,000 students.

In retrospect, the recommendations of the Strayer Report were understandably cautious. Faculty salaries were to be raised an average of 12.5 percent; at least $250,000 was needed for various improvements within the System and the strengthening of graduate education; and the Atlanta Division was to receive another $250,000 for needed improvements there. The sum of $80,000 would permit the Regents to add needed specialists to their central office staff.

To meet its financial needs, the University System should seek support from the state on the basis of "comprehensive plans looking to the future." Aid from philanthropy was also to be sought but not to the extent that it might reduce state support. Tuition was to be reduced to about 25 percent so that students paid a smaller proportion of their educational expenses. Housing, food, and other student services were to be improved but offered to students at a figure much closer to actual cost. And finally, if state support for current operations and capital outlay could be increased immediately to $13.2 million (an absolute increase of $7.7 million), the annual appropriation at this level should suffice until about 1958.

POSTWAR GROWTH

If the years 1946-1960 are regarded as the University System's second phase of development, they can be interpreted as a period in which the Board of Regents was actively concerned with the System's growth and expansion, campus planning and development, adequate funding, and the internal improvement of institutional programs and services. Policy making was not highly centralized, however, and most policy decisions were made on an *ad hoc* basis or in a piecemeal manner. Many decisions were based on informal studies and the recommendations of particular councils or committees who dealt with specific issues and problems.

In the early 1950s the Board of Regents was obviously concerned with the implementation of the major recommendations of the Strayer Report. The Georgia State Woman's College in Valdosta opened its doors to males and its title was changed to Valdosta State College. The University of Georgia School of Medicine became the Medical College of Georgia and was authorized to offer the master's degree in selected fields. The re-organization of agricultural programs in instruction, research, and cooperative extension was completed, and the functions of the State's three colleges for blacks were re-defined. Albany State College was designated as the State's liberal arts college for blacks, and the curricula at Albany State and Savannah

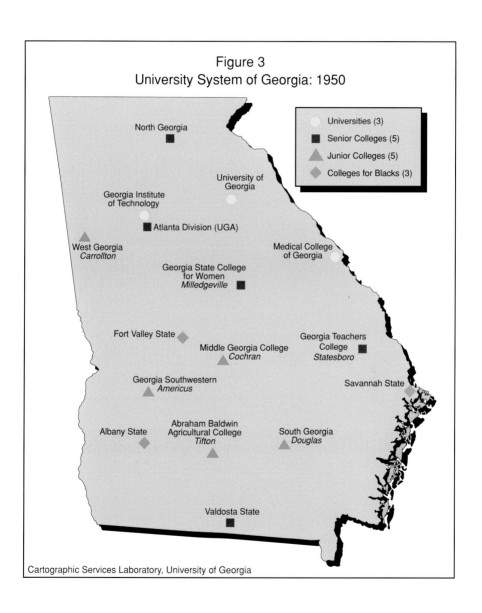

Figure 3
University System of Georgia: 1950

Universities (3)
Senior Colleges (5)
Junior Colleges (5)
Colleges for Blacks (3)

North Georgia

University of
Georgia

Georgia Institute
of Technology

Atlanta Division (UGA)

West Georgia
Carrollton

Medical College
of Georgia

Georgia State College
for Women
Milledgeville

Fort Valley State

Georgia Teachers
College
Statesboro

Middle Georgia College
Cochran

Georgia Southwestern
Americus

Savannah State

Abraham Baldwin
Agricultural College
Tifton

Albany State

South Georgia
Douglas

Valdosta State

State were altered to conform to the re-defined missions of the three institutions.

The size and status of the University System in 1950 are indicated by its 1,095 faculty members, a cumulative enrollment of 29,011 students, and 5,309 awarded degrees. The University of Georgia did not confer a Ph.D. in 1950 but Georgia Tech conferred *one*, along with 108 masters. The Atlanta Division of the University of Georgia conferred 72 Bachelor of Business Administration degrees and 242 Bachelors of Commercial Science. WWII veterans, taking advantage of the GI Bill, constituted 40 percent of the cumulative enrollment in 1949-1950.

During the next academic year the impact of the declining enrollment of veterans was severely felt when the cumulative enrollment declined 14.3 percent and a special allocation of $92,000 was necessary to cover the deficits resulting from departing veterans. For 1951-1952, however, state appropriations were raised to $12.3 million, more than twice the amount received in previous years. In implementing the recommendations of the Strayer Report, the borrowing limit of the University System Building Authority was increased from $12 million to $20 million, thereby enabling the Board of Regents to continue its building program. Long-range development studies were initiated during 1950-1951 and completed for nine institutions.

The number of University System faculty members declined in the early 1950s, but significant increases were observed in faculty members holding the Ph.D. and a significant reduction in the number of those holding only a bachelor's degree. In 1951-1952 the University of Georgia conferred three Ph.D.'s while Georgia Tech conferred two. Cumulative enrollments within the System were down 17.7 percent and the enrollment of veterans declined from 7,204 the previous year to 3,792 in FY52. The decline of *non-veteran* students was attributed, in part, to the addition of a twelfth grade by many Georgia high schools. When the number fell to 999 FTE faculty members in

FY52, the Board of Regents took steps to strengthen faculties by annual salaries that were 20 percent higher and by the adoption of uniform policies for: (a) appointment and promotion, (b) tenure, and (c) compulsory retirement at the age of 67 instead of 70 as in previous years.

Student enrollments continued to decline until 1954 when the beginning of an upward trend was noted by the Chancellor in his annual report. New degree programs were authorized at the doctoral level, research programs were improved, and significant changes in undergraduate programs were made.

EXTERNAL REVIEW AND STUDY

In 1955 the House of Representatives appointed a subcommittee to study the operations and needs of the University System. Members of the sub-committee were: J. Ebb Duncan, chairman; Mac Barber; Braswell Deen, Jr.; W.C. Massee; and Jack Murr. This study committee visited all units of the University System, interviewed campus officials, and prepared a report setting forth the conditions and needs of the various units. The committee recommended an annual appropriation of $23.7 million.

During 1955 the University System's inadequate financial support received extensive publicity in the Atlanta newspapers and a special session of the General Assembly was called for the purpose of raising additional revenue. The additional funds allocated to the Board of Regents in FY56 were $3.1 million.

Related to the State's increased support of higher education was the separation (September 1, 1955) of the Atlanta Division from the University of Georgia and the change of its title to the Georgia State College of Business Administration. Changes in institutional status had been recommended in the Second Works Report and the Strayer Report but needed the spur of new accreditation requirements adopted by the Southern Association in 1954.

OTHER SIGNIFICANT POLICY DECISIONS

The conversion of the Atlanta Division to Georgia State College was the first major change in institutional status during the 1950s. The Board of Regents moved (in 1956) their central offices from Georgia State to 244 Washington Street. Dr. Joseph E. Moore of Georgia Tech was temporarily appointed director of testing and guidance for the University System in 1956 and conducted a systemwide study of testing and guidance needs in public higher education. At its September 1956 meeting the Board adopted the College Board Scholastic Aptitude Test (SAT) as an admission requirement to units of the University System. Uses of the test by institutional officials were expected to "profoundly influence the institution's instructional program" (1956 *Annual Report*).

The National Defense Education Act of 1958 rekindled national interest in testing and counseling as it addressed the most pressing educational issues of identifying and training scientific, technical, and professional manpower. The Georgia Nuclear Advisory Commission, appointed by Governor Ernest Vandiver to study the impact of nuclear energy on the state's economic development, created four task forces to study: (a) testing, counseling, and guidance; (b) teacher education; (c) vocational education; and (d) educational television. Each task force prepared and published a report making recommendations to the Committee on Manpower and Education, chaired by William M. Suttles, dean of students at Georgia State. The staff director of these studies was Dr. Doak Campbell, president emeritus of Florida State University.

The reports on vocational and teacher education stressed the need for more extensive, improved programs that would meet the changing demands and expectations of society, but the report on educational television received the most attention from the public. Educational television was a far more appealing topic to the public and one that offered considerable promise for the future of education.

The task force on testing, counseling, and guidance was representative of the State's institutions of higher education, business and financial firms, and the State Health Department. The published report of the task force pointed to an expected college enrollment of 72,000 students in 1965, an increase of 71 percent over the recorded enrollment of students in 1955. To provide testing, counseling, and guidance for over 40,000 college students there were fewer than 30 professionally trained faculty or staff members in the entire state. An important recommendation, therefore, asked for a study of present facilities and programs for training counselors, one of the major provisions of the National Defense Education Act. Education and training programs should contain adequate coursework in testing and statistics as part of a minimum core for all teachers. Anticipated by this particular task force was an increased use in educational achievement tests, as well as aptitude tests, for college admissions. At least four institutions in 1959 already required College Board achievement tests, as well as the SAT. Also anticipated was widespread use of "high-speed electronic computers" for admission and placement decisions.

REGENTS OFFICE OF TESTING AND GUIDANCE

From its organization in 1957 to its demise in the late 1960s, the Regents Office of Testing and Guidance, under the direction of Dr. John R. Hills, provided a wealth of information to admission officers, counselors, and others concerned with the prediction of academic performance in units of the University System. An annual norms booklet was prepared in which SAT scores, high school grades, and college grades were analyzed for each of the institutions admitting students at the freshman level. By differentially weighting SAT-Verbal scores, SAT-Mathematics scores, and high school averages for its previous freshman class, prediction equations were developed for each institution. Included in each norms booklet was technical advice on the uses of predicted freshman grades for college admissions. Other publications of the Office provided assistance to high school counselors in their efforts to help individual students (*Counselor's Guide*, 1959).

An unusually informative feature of each norms booklet was the distributions, with means and standard deviations, of SAT scores and high school averages for all freshmen entering University System institutions. In the fall of 1958, for example, the average SAT-Verbal and SAT-Mathematics scores for 6,081 freshmen were 396 and 433, respectively. In high school these students had earned grades averaging 2.7 (on a 4.0 scale). In their freshman coursework they had earned slightly lower grade-point-averages, depending on the institution and the field of study. One of the additional benefits of the annual norms booklets was the encouragement given to more uniform grading practices in both high schools and colleges.

By 1960 the annual norms booklet had become a valuable source of information on the abilities and achievement of students entering the University System. Enrollment had increased to 7,297 students, and SAT scores with high school grades gave an excellent overview of student preparation for academic coursework at the college level. The mean high school average reported for freshmen was a "B" and the mean SAT scores of 427 on the verbal scale and 466 on the mathematics scale indicated substantial competencies in dealing with verbal and numerical concepts. A noticeable number of the entering freshmen scored below 400 on the verbal and mathematical scales, however, and only a relatively few scored above 600 on the two scales. In brief, no more than 5 percent of the entering freshmen displayed exceptional promise for academic coursework and roughly one-half of the group had verbal and mathematical abilities that suggested disadvantages in advanced or specialized work at the junior and senior levels. At least 10 percent of the 1960 entering freshmen had gained entrance to a unit of the University System with less than a "C" average.

The productivity of the staff is evidenced in other ways by the numerous journal articles and research bulletins published in the early 1960s. As other institutions in other states resorted to selective admissions as a means of coping with increased enrollments, the Regents' program became a model of statewide testing that received national attention. In addition to their research, the professional staff was quite active in workshops and conferences conducted for admission officers, counselors, and other student personnel workers. In each of these efforts there was innovation and leadership in developing a systemwide testing program and a statewide concern with student advisement, guidance, and counseling.

SELECTIVE ADMISSIONS

As college applications increased in the late 1950s, many colleges adopted higher admission standards as a means of controlling course enrollments and the increasing demands placed on college faculties and facilities. In particular, institutions with limited facilities and little room for expansion turned to selective admissions as a way of maintaining traditional images and missions. Institutions with unfilled classrooms and dormitories responded in a different manner.

As a centrally located institution with limited opportunities and resources for expansion, Georgia State College developed in 1959 a selective admissions program that contrasted sharply with its previous reputation as an open-door evening school. Under a court injunction not to discriminate against minority applicants and under state laws that: (a) limited the age of first-time college entrants and (b) withheld all funds in the event of court-ordered integration, Georgia State was, in many respects, the University System's "experiment station" for selective admissions. The admission procedures developed and followed from 1959 until 1965 are still instructive in their implications for institutions enforcing higher academic standards in the admission process.

In addition to the SAT which was already required for entering freshmen, Georgia State applicants were required to take an extensive series of academic ability and educational achievement tests. Included in the "battery" of tests were measures of vocabulary, reading comprehension, and general achievement in natural science, mathematics, and social studies. Also required in the admissions process was an interview with a panel of three faculty members who made recommendations independent of the applicant's test performance. For admission as an entering freshmen, only applicants who had followed a college preparatory course in high school were eligible. Four units in English and two units in mathematics, each with a "C or better" average grade, were mandatory.

The effectiveness of the new admission standards was documented in a doctoral dissertation by Thomas F. McDonald (1966). Statistically significant increases in SAT scores and high school averages were clearly evident, and appreciable improvement in academic performance was suggested by freshman grades. There were considerable variations in faculty grading practices, however, and the average grades recorded for introductory grades suggested a persistence in faculty expectations of student achievement. In brief, the "rapid transition" to selective admissions had produced significant changes in student characteristics, but corresponding changes in faculty expectations and grading practices were not evident for several years. During the 1960s Georgia State changed in dramatic ways its institutional reputation and mission, but its success was not as much a function of selective admissions as its rapid expansion of degree programs to meet the increasing demand for higher education in a rapidly growing urban area.

EXPANSION OF GEORGIA'S JUNIOR COLLEGES

In 1957 a special committee of the General Assembly studied the State's need for additional junior colleges and recommended the passage of legislation that would permit local government agencies to establish and operate new junior colleges. The ensuing Junior College Act of 1958 provided for a system of junior colleges that would be established and operated by local authority—and not as units of the University System. The Board of Regents, however, was authorized to adopt rules and regulations by which the local operating authorities would receive state aid (Georgia Laws, 1958 Session, pp. 47-50). DeKalb Community College, the only college established under the Junior College Act of 1958, received in its first years of operation a stipend of $300 for each student enrolled.

The enactment of the 1958 Junior College Act was a sharp spur to the Board of Regents in their commitment to the expansion of educational opportunity. Following studies of educational needs in Augusta, Savannah, and Columbus the Regents negotiated with: (a) the Richmond County Board of Education for the transfer of its junior college to the University System, (b) the City of Savannah for the transfer of Armstrong College, and (c) the Muscogee County School District for the creation of a new junior college. Thus Augusta College and Armstrong College, two previously established (and locally controlled) institutions, became units of the University System. One, Augusta College, had been founded in 1925 as a county-operated junior college while the other, Armstrong College, had an equally interesting history as a city-owned junior college founded in 1935 and housed in a historic Savannah mansion. The third unit, Columbus College, became the first newly established institution since the creation of the University System Center. The operation of the new colleges required a special allocation of $400,000 to the Board of Regents, and each entered the University System "by virtue of the authority of the Board of Regents" (1958 *Annual Report*) and not as instruments of the Junior College Act.

As the decade of the 1950s drew to a close, the institutional composition of the University System was: (a) four "comprehensive" institutions, (b) five senior colleges enrolling whites, (c) three senior colleges enrolling blacks, and (d) seven junior colleges. The addition of three junior colleges brought the total to nineteen units and the geographical distribution of institutions thereby increased educational opportunity.

The enrollment of 30,686 students had been restricted, however, by the passage of the Age-Limit Law of 1959. The law, passed without consultation with academic leaders, placed restrictions on the enrollment of undergraduates over 21 years of age and the admission of graduate students over twenty-five. The number of University System faculty members in 1960 was 1,512, an increase of 46 over the previous year. The average salary paid to teaching faculty on a nine-months contract was $5,973—an increase of 64.1 percent from the $3,639 paid in the academic year of 1949-1950. The University of Georgia, having conferred one Ph.D. in 1950, conferred 12 Ph.D.'s in l960, along with 8 Ed.D.'s; Georgia Tech conferred 12 Ph.D.'s that year.

If the immediate postwar years (1946-1950) are perceived as a period of readjustment in which the G.I. Bill was a dominant influence in a statewide quest for educational self-sufficiency, the 1950s can be regarded as years in which the University System also made progress toward educational respectability. Throughout the decade the University System's enrollments grew at an annual rate of 6.7 percent while the State's population increased from 3.4 million to 3.9 million (an annual increase of 1.4%). By 1960 the University System had an additional 12,269 students distributed among its various units. The increase in enrollments for the decade was 67 percent higher than the University System's enrollment in 1950.

In retrospect the postwar years of 1946-1960 should be viewed as a period of growth, expansion, and change in which commendable efforts were made to improve educational opportunities within the University System. The Regents and other state leaders were influenced by a changing "philosophy of education" that was expressed best by the President's Commission on Higher Education (1947). American colleges and universities were challenged to envision a larger and more significant role for higher education in the national life. Higher education was no longer a privilege for an intellectual elite but the means by which the nation's citizens could realize their individual potential for personal growth and development. From its perspective the Commission was convinced that at least half of the nation's college-age youth could benefit from two years of college. To that end the Commission addressed ways in which campus facilities could be expanded, technical institutes could be established, and college curricula could be improved.

A pronounced emphasis was placed on higher education as the means by which human talents could be discovered and developed. Testing and counseling were embraced as the means by which the various talents of students could be identified, appraised, fostered, and encouraged—and education was the means by which they could be developed and used. Guidance centers had proven effective for returning military veterans and many colleges followed suit in establishing offices of testing and counseling. A national interest in educational and vocational counseling (and placement) was thereby spurred—and with the passage of the National Defense Education Act of 1958, the discovery and development of talent was given the blessings and support of public policy. Accompanying this movement was an extensive national concern for college and university faculties, their formal preparation, working conditions, and the meager salaries. Many institutions responded with efforts to upgrade their faculties and to improve job benefits and working conditions. The gist of such changes was an increasing awareness of institutions, students, and faculties as public resources that required public attention and better financial support.

CHAPTER FOUR

Growth and Expansion: 1960-1972

Georgians today, whether or not they realize it, are fighting the educational battles of the 1970's. The outcome will depend largely upon their actions during the next two or three years. The outcome of the battles of the 1960's is already determined by the actions and inactions of the past.
Governor's Commission To Improve Education, 1963

The institutional composition of the University System changed dramatically in the 1960s, a decade of unprecedented growth, expansion, and progress. In 1964 the increased birthrate that began in 1946 was evident on all college campuses as eighteen-year-olds graduated from high school in unprecedented numbers and enrolled in college the following fall. Georgians were no exception to the national trend, and by the end of the decade neither the overall structure nor functions of higher education was the same nationally, regionally, or locally. Old institutions re-defined their mission and role. New institutions opened as rapidly as the construction of campus facilities would permit—and more than a few colleges began in temporary quarters while awaiting the completion of construction.

In December 1961 Georgia State was permitted to drop the prepositional phrase "of Business Administration" from its title and offer master of arts degrees in English, history, and political science. Also authorized at that time were a master of arts degree for teachers and a master of business education degree.

In 1963 new junior colleges were approved for Albany-Dougherty County, Dalton-Whitefield County, and Marietta-Cobb County. Approval of these three colleges was followed in 1964 by authorization of a fourth new college in Gainesville-Hall County. Beginning in 1963 the Regents began the upgrading of four junior colleges into senior institutions. Augusta College was granted permission to offer senior-division work in 1965, and Armstrong College would offer similar work in 1966. Both colleges were permitted to add additional years of academic coursework as an entering freshman class progressed in its studies. In this way, the junior year was added one year prior to the addition of the senior year. In early 1964 Georgia Southwestern was accorded the same privilege and was scheduled to offer upper-division work in 1966. During the 1964-1965 academic year Columbus College received permission to upgrade its status beginning in 1968 and conferred its first bachelor's degrees in 1970. As documented in a later doctoral dissertation (Denning, 1972), the four institutions were successful in their relatively easy transition to senior college status, but changes in institutional status were not as evident in student characteristics as they were in faculty credentials and program structure.

The status of the University System in the 1963-1964 academic year is significant because of the numerous changes that most institutions of higher education experienced in the fall of 1964 and the years thereafter. On June 30, 1964 the institutional composition of the University System was the same as it had been since the opening of Columbus College. During the academic year of 1963-1964, however, a total of 1,826 faculty members taught the full-time-equivalent of 30,575 students enrolled in nineteen institutions. For their teaching, University System faculty members received an average salary of $7,589, an increase of $217 over the previous year. The University of Georgia conferred 35 Ph.D.'s and 16 Ed.D.'s while Georgia Tech conferred 25 Ph.D.'s in several fields of engineering.

The dramatic increase in University System enrollments in 1964 was not unexpected, but it was not properly anticipated. Georgians did not participate in higher education at the same rate as residents of other states and although it was evident from high school graduation rates that more students were completing high school, it was not anticipated that a higher proportion of those graduates would enroll in college. In a two-year period (1964-65) the number of high school graduates increased almost

40 percent. No other event, perhaps, could have demonstrated so well the University System's need for statewide planning and development.

The number of freshmen entering the University System in 1964 was over ten thousand, an increase of at least 38 percent since 1960. The 1964 freshman class was the first of the postwar generation to enter college, and their better preparation was evident in the higher proportion who scored above 600 on the SAT-Verbal or SAT-Mathematics scales. An appreciable increase was also observed in the mid-range (400-600) where the majority of entering freshmen were expected to score. At least 13 percent of the class entered with an "A" average in high school. Also evident in 1964 was the increased enrollment of minority students in the University System. Their relative participation did not increase, however, to the same extent noted for majority students.

PROGRAM PLANNING AND DEVELOPMENT

In 1961 the University System of Georgia agreed to co-sponsor with the Georgia State Department of Education and the Georgia Department of Public Health a study of the State's need for nurses and other paramedical personnel. Work on a statewide survey began in October 1961 and was concluded the following year in the same month. Included in the survey were twelve occupations regarded as essential to adequate health care for Georgia residents: (1) dietitian, (2) hospital administrator, (3) laboratory technician, (4) licensed practical nurse, (5) medical assistant, (6) medical records librarian, (7) medical social worker, (8) medical technologist, (9) occupational therapist, (10) physical therapist, (11) registered nurse, and (12) X-ray technician. The purpose of the survey was to determine present and future needs for such personnel and to evaluate the adequacy of educational and training programs for meeting those needs (Fincher, 1962).

The survey was most effective in verifying the State's need for health care personnel. The demand for health and medical

services was definitely increasing and there were critical shortages in nursing and paramedical occupations. Educational and
training programs were inadequate to meet present needs and
certainly could not meet future needs. Nowhere in Georgia were
there programs for preparing dietitians, medical assistants, medical social workers, occupational therapists, or physical therapists. Personnel for the remaining occupations were variously
prepared for their duties by an array of hospital schools, vocational schools, and public or private colleges.

Recommendations to the sponsoring agencies included the
establishment of accredited programs where there were none,
the improvement of inadequate or weak programs, and the full-
est possible coordination of existing and future educational
and training programs. To provide adequate health and medical
care to its residents, the State needed an effective statewide system
of recruitment and placement, better advisement and counseling
services in its schools and colleges, and more effective policies
for utilization of nursing and paramedical personnel.

The nursing and paramedical survey was favorably received.
Directly related to survey findings was the establishment of
the State Scholarship Commission as a means of providing financial aid to students enrolling in critical-need professional
programs. Instead of responding merely to the nursing and paramedical needs documented for twelve specific occupations, the
sponsoring agencies made recommendations to the General
Assembly legislation that would provide a general canopy for
state assistance. Also related was the development of the schools
of allied health services at Georgia State and the Medical College,
and intensified efforts on the part of the allied health fields, as
they quickly became known, in recruitment and public relations.
A later modification of state laws permitted the licensing of
graduates from two-year collegiate schools of nursing. This change
enabled University System junior colleges to establish nursing
programs and contribute to the supply of professional nurses.

REGENTS STUDY OF HIGHER EDUCATION

In April 1963 the Board of Regents authorized a statewide study of higher education in Georgia. Dr. S. Walter Martin, vice chancellor of the University System, was designated director of the study and chairman of a nine-member steering committee. Thomas W. Mahler, associate director of the Georgia Center for Continuing Education, was selected as associate director of the study. Six task forces were organized to consider: (1) the scope and functions of post-high school education; (2) junior colleges and area trade schools; (3) demographic forces affecting the demand for higher education; (4) the planning and coordination of junior colleges; (5) estimated costs and finances; and (6) educational programs for science, professions, and technology.

The task force on educational programs was asked to consider present and future needs for degree-granting programs. Its original charge was then broadened to include the State's resources and needs for institutional research and to maintain close liaison with the task force on scope and functions. Dr. Judson C. Ward, Jr., vice president of Emory University and former president of Georgia Southern, was appointed chairman.

An early announcement by Vice Chancellor Martin to the task force on educational programs was the news that Emory, Georgia Tech, and the University of Georgia would confer, in 1963, a combined total of 100 PhDs. The University of Georgia conferred 20 PhDs and 14 EdDs but its cumulative total of conferred doctoral degrees had not yet reached a hundred. Also among the initial findings was an urgent need for cooperation among the state's three doctoral-granting institutions but a recognition that cooperation was not highly probable.

The Regents Study of Higher Education was discontinued in the summer of 1963 when Governor Carl Sanders commissioned the Governor's Commission To Improve Education. When relevant, the work of the Regents task forces was absorbed by the larger, more extensive, better funded study. Thomas W. Mahler was appointed associate director of the professional staff assembled for the Commission's purposes and would continue his study of higher education, as launched by the Regents. James L. Miller, Jr., director of research at Southern Regional Education Board (SREB), was granted leave to serve as director and Woodrow W. Breland, professor of education at Georgia State, was appointed associate director for elementary and secondary education.

GOVERNOR'S COMMISSION TO IMPROVE EDUCATION

The Commission study authorized by Governor Sanders was the first comprehensive study of elementary, secondary, vocational-technical, and higher education in Georgia. An excellent professional staff and ample resources were made available for consideration and study of educational issues at all levels. Governor Sanders served as chairman of the Governor's Commission and placed the major emphasis of his administration on the improvement of education and the closing of educational gaps that embarrassed the State.

The Commission adopted the goals stated by the SREB Commission on Goals (1962) and worked within the context of ten objectives specifically related to Georgia's educational needs. The objectives addressed the issues of improvement and equality in educational opportunity, minimum standards for public schools, balanced academic and occupational programs, the recruitment and retention of good teachers, the improvement of efficiency, a statewide television network, planning and research, and adequate financial support for public schools and colleges.

Representation on the Commission was appreciative of social, economic, and cultural forces within the State. On the Commission were two future governors of Georgia and one future president of the United States; a future lieutenant governor; several highly visible opinion leaders; and several future members of the Board of Regents itself. Although politics and race were much involved, the Commission, much to its credit, kept its sights on its educational objectives.

The strongest recommendations in the report dealt with planning. The Commission stated unequivocably that the "most important single prerequisite for educational improvement in Georgia [was] effective long-range planning" (p. 18). Such planning should be continuous and could not be the work of a single commission. For the Board of Regents, the report emphasized a "top priority need" for a research and planning unit to identify and define "long-range problems and needs" (p. 49). For the separate units of the University System there was a need for institutional research offices. For the University System as a whole there was a need for "comprehensive community junior college(s) . . . by which local and community needs should be met." These colleges "should be established on the basis of a statewide survey using the best criteria known . . . [and] on a priority schedule over a period of years" (p. 52).

The Commission noted as one of its most difficult problems the relationships between community colleges and vocational-technical schools. The Commission recommended continued jurisdiction by the Regents in areas where there were junior colleges and no vocational-technical schools but "memoranda of agreement" with the State Board of Education in areas where both types of institutions existed. Noting that junior colleges had already been approved for Albany, Brunswick, Dalton, and Marietta, the Commission recommended joint experimentation with comprehensive community colleges in areas where neither vocational-technical schools nor junior colleges existed. A particular emphasis was placed on "close cooperation and coordination" between the two statewide boards of education. To this end, both boards should take immediate action "to accomplish whatever changes are necessary in policy, organization, and staffing" to devote to long-range planning. The boards, themselves, should meet jointly on matters of mutual concern.

A major emphasis, as would be expected, was on elementary and secondary education and the adequacy of their financing. The subtitle, "Investment in the Future", is indicative of the emphasis given education as an investment and the return-on-investment to society. Such an investment "will require full financial support from both state and local sources" and "every dollar's worth of wealth in Georgia should pay its fair share..." (p. 72). The challenge called for "leadership of the highest order" and "educational innovation and experimentation."

In dealing with the State's efforts to attract space age industry, the Commission recognized the tardiness of its major universities in organized research and graduate education. Attention was called to the State's shortage of scientific, professional, and technical personnel in areas of sponsored research related to the space age and to the need for "a generally higher level of educational attainment" (p.72). Basic research was acknowledged as "a function of the state's universities" but for reasons unknown, the Commission's recommendations for graduate education are the weakest in its report.

The findings and recommendations of the Governor's Commission To Improve Education report were widely publicized and endorsed. Results were not always immediate but they were substantive. One significant outcome was the formation of the Georgia Educational Improvement Council, an intergovernmental agency consisting of representatives of the State Board of Education, the Board of Regents, the General Assembly, and private enterprise. Thomas W. Mahler was appointed the first executive director of this agency and continued many of the cooperative efforts initiated by, or recommended by, the Governor's Commission. When Governor Jimmy Carter decided to abolish this agency as an executive arm, the staff was reassigned to the General Assembly as a legislative agency.

The urgency of the Commission's work was dramatized one year later when the number of high school graduates in the state increased by 19.1 percent and an increased proportion enrolled in units of the University System. The year 1964, as often pointed out, was the first year of the "impending tidal wave" discussed by Roland B. Thompson of Ohio State in various national publications.

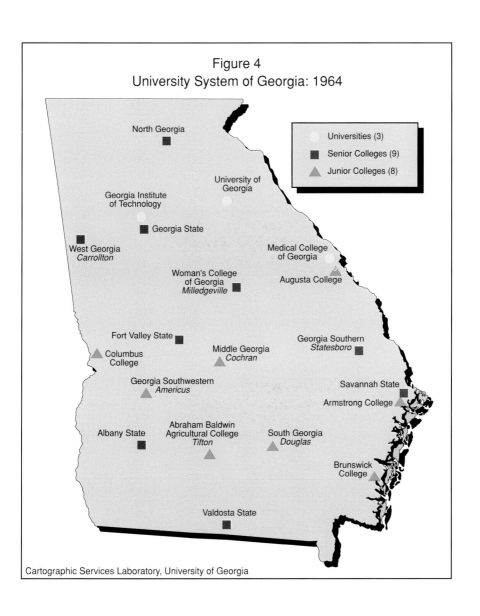

Figure 4
University System of Georgia: 1964

North Georgia

Universities (3)
Senior Colleges (9)
Junior Colleges (8)

University of Georgia

Georgia Institute of Technology

Georgia State

West Georgia
Carrollton

Medical College of Georgia

Woman's College of Georgia
Milledgeville

Augusta College

Fort Valley State

Georgia Southern
Statesboro

Columbus College

Middle Georgia
Cochran

Georgia Southwestern
Americus

Savannah State

Armstrong College

Albany State

Abraham Baldwin Agricultural College
Tifton

South Georgia
Douglas

Brunswick College

Valdosta State

Cartographic Services Laboratory, University of Georgia

Other outcomes of the Governor's Commission report were less visible. The report and the Governor's Conference on Education, called to publicize the Commission's findings, were undoubtedly effective in calling attention to educational needs and in committing more of the state's resources to education. What the work of the Governor's Commission demonstrated best, no doubt, was the need for effective leadership!

REGENTS STUDY OF COMMUNITY JUNIOR COLLEGES

One important recommendation of the Governor's Commission was implemented the following year (1964) when the Regents directed the Chancellor to conduct a comprehensive study of the need for additional junior colleges and to recommend their locations. This action was apparently triggered by the approval in March 1964 of Gainesville Junior College, which was the fifth junior college approved by the Regents since 1958.

In 1963 the Regents requested a study of the northwestern corner of the state that resulted in the approval of Dalton and Kennesaw junior colleges. That study was conducted in response to petitions from five different communities in the Seventh Congressional District for junior colleges and the Regents were obviously under the pressure of "planning by chambers of commerce."

The Governor's Commission responded to the particular issue, in effect, by saying the planning should be done on a systematic, statewide basis and as "a function of the Board of Regents." With this reminder of their responsibilities, the Regents responded by appointing an eight-member advisory committee which included representatives of Georgia colleges and universities who were well informed about national and regional trends in the development of higher education. Consultants for the study were B. Lamar Johnson from UCLA and I.E. Ready, head of the Community College Division of the North Carolina Department of Instruction. Staff directors of the study were S. Walter Martin, vice chancellor and later acting chancellor, and Harry S. Downs, coordinator of junior colleges in the University System.

The premises on which the study was conducted were: (a) equal and more-or-less universal opportunity for education beyond the high school; (b) acceptance of community colleges as comprehensive postsecondary institutions; (c) the essentialness of long-range planning; (d) Georgia's need for its own plan; (e) operation of community colleges by the Board of Regents; (f) a fixed role for community colleges as community colleges; (g) the need to identify communities and to recommend locations; (h) consideration of vocational-technical schools and their role; (i) the avoidance of needless duplication; (j) the study to serve as a foundation for future and continuing studies; (k) smooth articulation between schools and colleges, including community college/senior college transfers; and (l) the expectation that community colleges would increase rates of participation.

Among the guidelines established for the study were: (a) a potential enrollment of more than 400 students; (b) an acceptable concentration of population; (c) a commuting radius of 35 miles; and (d) community desire, interest, and ability to finance. Locations were to be assigned either a Priority A: "immediate development . . . seems justified," or a Priority B: "potentially promising [but] should continue to be studied. . . ."

The locations assigned a Priority A were four in number. To the study committee's satisfaction, community colleges were needed in the Bibb and Houston counties area, in the downtown area of Atlanta, on the west side of Atlanta, and in the south Atlanta area. Georgia State was identified as the logical institution to assume community college responsibilities in the downtown Atlanta area and Atlanta Junior College was the eventual outcome of the priority assigned western Atlanta. The Bibb/Houston priority, however, was an impediment in the study committee's report. Political commitments apparently had been made to Bibb County and the study committee was asked to make its recommendation specific. The study committee, believing the political commitment premature and thinking it had done enough in specifying the area, did not believe it could, in good conscience, recommend only Bibb County. Consequently, the final report was mimeographed only as a staff report for internal use by the University System.

ROLE AND SCOPE STUDY OF USGA INSTITUTIONS

Another recommendation to which the Board of Regents responded was "a comprehensive study of the appropriate role of each institution within the University System and the appropriate scope of its activities" (p. 50). Such a study was launched in 1965 following the appointment of Dr. George L. Simpson, Jr. as chancellor. Dr. Walter Martin, vice chancellor of the University System, was designated study director and the Institute of Higher Education at the University of Georgia, then in its second year of operations, provided the staff work. The Chancellor and the Board of Regents requested that the study be concluded by June 30, 1966.

The Institute staff defined the premises upon which a role and scope study should be conducted and the information needed from the separate institutions. There was agreement that: (a) the demand for higher education would increase; (b) the majority of Georgia college students would continue to enroll in the University System; (c) meeting the increased demand would require both an expansion of academic programs and adequate planning and coordination; and (d) all units of the University System must assume a role that would be part of a larger whole.

An essential part of the study was the specification of general guidelines under which institutional and program development should take place. These guidelines were specified at the outset and took into consideration the University System's need for expanded educational opportunities that would be in keeping with the resources of the State and the capabilities of

its institutions. For examples, the Ph.D. should not be offered
in any one academic field at more than two universities and professional programs (such as law, pharmacy, and social work)
should be significantly improved before diverting resources
into new programs. The development of programs in the Atlanta and Athens areas should be cognizant of their proximity,
as well as the increasing concentration of the state's population.
Other guidelines dealt with considerations of the requirements
of national and regional accreditation, evidence of need and
demand, and the tri-fold mission of junior colleges.

In identifying the institutional role of each unit of the University System, a careful review of each institution's historical
development, the scope and diversity of its current programs,
and its institutional mission (as perceived by the president)
suggested at least six functional institutional roles for the diversified units of the University System. Four of the institutions already served the major functions for which universities
are traditionally known; three of the senior colleges had a regional role (in their provision of limited graduate work); five of
the senior colleges were limited in their efforts to define new
roles by historical traditions; three senior colleges (by virtue of
their location) had community ties that defined many of their
responsibilities; and the junior colleges differed significantly
in their community services and whether or not they attracted
students from outside their immediate area.

A disappointing outcome of the role and scope study was
the license taken by many institutions in projecting academic
programs for future development. Student enrollments, full-
time faculty, and credit-hours taught had shown a remarkable
unevenness across institutions but the institutional aspirations
of many units were inordinate. In short, the guidelines developed for the study could not curb the desires and preferences of
administrative staffs and faculties.

Given its premises, its guidelines, and the cooperation of
participating institutions, the role and scope study of the University System could have served as an informed guide to future

institutional and program development. The six institutional roles defined in the study, however, were either politically or budgetarily unacceptable and despite sound caution in the study's conclusions and recommendations, the scope of academic programs under the canopy of institutional role was undoubtedly seen as opening floodgates of institutional aspirations already out of hand.

A long range planning study began a few months after the role and scope study was completed. The staff work for this study was provided by members of the Chancellor's central staff and each institution was asked to specify its own assumptions concerning enrollments, entrance requirements, academic programs, faculty, facilities, and other institutional activities. For example, an assumption made for the University of Georgia was that it would continue to enroll approximately 25 percent of the equivalent-full-time on-campus enrollment in the University System. Also assumed were such matters as the continued recruitment and retention of well qualified faculty, the expansion of research programs, and "a major break-through in graduate education."

Definitions were provided by the Chancellor's staff for data elements that were to be projected for 1970-71 and 1975-76. Twelve categories were given for projections in educational and general expenditures while nine categories were given for educational and general income. For example, the FY75 E&G expenditures for the University of Georgia were projected to exceed one million dollars, a tripling of its actual expenditures in 1965-66. As another example, the University of Georgia faculty was expected to reach 1,500 in the academic year of 1970-71, a figure that was attained at least two years earlier.

For the University System, the planning projections were put to effective use in 1967 by Chancellor George Simpson in his budgetary requests for the 1967-69 Biennium. In a public statement entitled, "A Dam Has Broken," Chancellor Simpson made a persuasive appeal for funds that would permit the University System to meet its obviously increasing obligations.

POLICY DECISIONS IN 1960-1972

The decade of the 1960s can be viewed as years in which the State's first serious efforts were made in statewide planning for higher education. The development of the University System during the 1950s was commendable but piecemeal. No system-wide policies guided or directed the growth and expansion of higher education, and too many policy decisions were made by state legislators and other public leaders who proposed institutional and program changes to the Board of Regents.

The 1962 nursing and paramedical survey was the first state-wide effort to plan and develop academic programs on the basis of systematic research into the supply and demand of professionally trained personnel. The Regents Study of Higher Education was the first concerted effort to view the total picture of higher education within the State and to include representation of private higher education on all six task forces. The Sanders Commission To Improve Education was the only statewide, public commission to consider education from kindergarten to graduate school. And the Regents Study of Community Junior Colleges was the Board of Regents' first recognition that within its own institutions could be found the knowledge and expertise needed to fashion a plan for the orderly development of two-year colleges.

Despite the fact that decisions and commitments for Brunswick, Gainesville, Kennesaw, and Albany junior colleges had been made in the early 1960s, their construction and development were influenced by the concerted efforts to plan and direct the growth of higher education in the 1964-1972 period. It is most relevant that between 1964 and 1972, eight new junior colleges opened their doors and provided additional access and educational opportunity to Georgians in a period of rapid growth and expansion. Macon Junior and Clayton Junior colleges were undoubtedly proposed and approved as a result of the Regents Study of Community Junior Colleges. Although Atlanta Junior College did not open until 1974, it too was the result of planning carried out in the mid-1960s. In much the same manner,

Floyd Junior College (although given a "B" priority in 1964) was an outcome of both the 1964 study and the earlier study of northwest Georgia. The approval of all three colleges had been made at a time *when* a climate for growth and expansion prevailed and *before* student protests in 1968 and 1970 resulted in a severe climatic change for higher education nationally.

The Board of Regents' commitment to the expansion of educational opportunity still prevailed in December 1970 when approval was given to six additional sites for junior colleges. It is relevant that the study by which the six new locations were identified was conducted internally by the Chancellor's staff. The sites were: (1) Bainbridge-Decatur County, (2) Dublin-Laurens County, (3) Griffin-Spalding County, (4) Swainsboro-Emanuel County, (5) Thomasville-Thomas County, and (6) Waycross-Ware County. Approval was given on the basis that despite the escalation of four institutions to senior college status, the State's two-year colleges had continued to educate approximately 14 percent of all students enrolled in the University System. Also relevant were projections of continued increased enrollment during the 1970s and prospects of community readiness to fund and support junior colleges in the six locations. Bond issues for site acquisition and construction were defeated in Laurens County (February 1973), Spalding County (June 1971), and Thomas County (August 1973) but local support was forthcoming at the other three sites and resulted in Bainbridge, Emanuel County, and Waycross junior colleges.

Among the decisive changes in the 1960-1972 period was the desegregation of the University System's predominantly white institutions and the changing status and functions of Albany State, Fort Valley State, and Savannah State colleges. With the admission of Hamilton Holmes and Charlayne Hunter to the University of Georgia in 1961 the Board of Regents was no longer impaled on the horns of conflicting federal and state laws. The Regents and institutions of the University System would continue to be involved in court cases and federal regulations dealing with desegregation, but they were no longer subject to state laws that threatened institutional closure. With the passage of Title III of the Higher Education Act of 1965 (and other federal legislation of the era) the three public colleges for blacks received public endorsement of their mission and role as essential public resources. The nation's "predominantly black colleges and universities" were first identified as a national resource in a study by Earl McGrath (1965), a former U.S. Commissioner of Education. McGrath's study was instrumental in creating a climate of public opinion in which institutional assistance was seen as being in the national interest.

Albany State, Fort Valley State, and Savannah State benefited in numerous ways from the changes in public policy. The presidents, deans, and faculties were increasingly involved in statewide conferences, inter-institutional meetings, and academic councils. For the first time they participated fully in administrative and academic decisions concerning the University System's development. Title III funds were particularly effective in helping the three institutions develop long range plans, offices of institutional research, and campus information systems. With other federal and state funds, Title III was also instrumental in the improvement of undergraduate programs, the addition of graduate work, the professional development of faculty, the improvement of instruction, and the enhancement of student services. A special benefit, according to one study, was the opportunities provided for the professional development of institutional leaders (Fincher, 1980).

Other significant events during the years between 1964 and 1972 were: (a) the creation of the Georgia State Scholarship Commission and the Georgia Higher Education Assistance Corporation by the General Assembly in 1965, (b) efforts to establish "special-help" programs for students not fully qualified for college coursework, (c) special funds to university-level institutions to assist in the development of academic departments of distinction, (d) the adoption in 1967 of a new transfer credit plan and/or core curriculum, (e) the addition in 1967 of several hundred new faculty positions that raised the University System total to 3,543 faculty members, and (f) the escalation of Southern Tech to a four-year division authorized to confer a bachelor of engineering technology degree.

Regents' policies and decisions during the 1960s were influenced profoundly by the radical demands and expectations that characterized the decade. Unprecedented growth and expansion, the stimulus of federal legislation and financial assistance, the difficulties of accommodating massive enrollments, the disruptions of student protests, the growing dissatisfaction of private benefactors, and the waning of public support often obscured the substantive and enduring progress that was made during the decade. The Higher Education Act of 1965 was a positive and constructive force in the development of institutions, programs, and professional personnel. Without the stimulus and challenge given by federal legislation, the growth and expansion of educational opportunities would have taken other directions with a different kind of momentum.

In summary—from 1964 to 1972 the University System gained each year an additional 8,028 students, the equivalent of four junior colleges with enrollments of 2,000 students each. The average annual increase of 18 percent expanded enrollments to over 100,000 students by 1971 and to 108,779 students the following year. With the opening of Floyd Junior College in 1970, the University System consisted of 27 institutions of public higher education and educational opportunities were within commuting distance of 90 percent of the State's (4.5 million) population.

For many reasons—1964, 1968, and 1970 must be regarded as pivotal and traumatic years in American higher education. Student protests on Georgia campuses were relatively mild when compared to those in other states, but Georgia colleges and universities were undeniably affected. In particular the shock of student protests was severe for campus administrators, faculty members, and alumni who knew nothing of student dissent until it was reported on the evening news. In virtually all respects, the 1960s closed on a pessimistic note that contrasts sharply with the decade's initial enthusiasm. The outlook for the University System in 1972 was not as encouraging or promising as it had been in 1960, *but* a larger and improved system of public higher education was in place and its institutions were much better staffed and equipped to serve the educational needs of Georgians.

CHAPTER FIVE
Reform and Consolidation: 1972-1984

Most of the people born during the "baby boom" years did not go to college. Now, many years later, those people are of middle age; and many of them are contemplating the advantages which a college education, if obtained even at this time, would confer on them. We witness a "greying" of the students at a number of our institutions.
Chancellor Vernon Crawford, *1980 Annual Report*

The year 1972 was indeed a decisive turning point in American higher education. The disruptive years of 1966-1970 severely undermined public confidence in higher education, its institutions, its faculties, and its students. From the heights of the early 1960s public opinion concerning the effectiveness of American colleges and universities descended to its lowest depths. With such change in public perceptions came drastic changes in public demands and expectations—and many changes in public policy!

The Educational Amendments of 1972 depict, in both subtle and obvious ways, the changing demands and expectations placed upon higher education in the aftermath of the 1960s. As a revision of the historic legislation of the mid-1960s, the Educational Amendments Act was both progressive and reactionary in its alteration of funding policies and practices and in its expressions of public perceptions, expectations, and concerns. Among the many changes in public policy were forms of direct financial assistance for students that would permit students to enroll in institutions of their preference. Instead of supporting institutions and programs, in implementation of public policy, the amendments directed national priorities to basic and supplementary grants for "low income and minority" students. Other changes were equivalent to a redefinition of higher education as an instrument of national policy. Public higher education and private higher education were joined with vocational-technical schools and proprietary institutions to comprise four sectors of postsecondary education.

Funding priorities were altered accordingly. Low income and minority students were designated as recipients of study loans, as participants in work-study programs, and as beneficiaries of special programs, such as Talent Search, Upward Bound, Special Services, and Educational Opportunity Centers. Title III (for developing institutions) remained intact as the only form of "general" institutional support but the criteria for Title III funds excluded the great majority of colleges. Throughout the amendments, policies and priorities emphasized planning, management, and evaluation. The clear implication of such emphases was the widespread belief that American colleges and universities has been mismanaged and that public policy should foster the adoption of modern management techniques in institutional operations.

Within the University System the early 1970s may be regarded as years of readjustment and accommodation, as well as years in which strenuous efforts were made to consolidate the gains of the 1960s. Having extended educational opportunity through the geographical distribution of institutions, the University System in the late 1970s sought extension of educational opportunities through program planning and development. As new and conflicting demands were placed upon its institutions of higher learning, the University System sought ways in which it could strengthen its programs and services for its many new constituencies and its diverse clientele.

During the 1971-1972 academic year Armstrong State, Augusta, Columbus, Georgia Southwestern, and Albany State colleges were authorized to offer graduate work at the master's level and North Georgia College was approved as a resident graduate center. In September 1971 authority for the operation of Gordon Military College was passed to the Board of Regents and in 1972 Gordon Junior College became the 28th unit of the University System. In the fall of 1973 Bainbridge Junior and

Emanuel County Junior colleges raised the number of institutions to 30. In 1974 Atlanta Junior College became the 31st. During the same year a feasibility study for an additional college was conducted in Gwinnett County, a special committee was appointed to study tenure, and a new law school was authorized for Georgia State. Role and scope studies were initiated for senior institutions within the System with expectations that a role and scope study would be conducted for the entire University System.

In 1975-1976 the Board of Regents placed a new emphasis on inter-institutional programs within the System and underscored quality and efficiency in the State's many health care programs. Kennesaw Junior College was authorized to upgrade its status to a senior college in the fall of 1978. A short-fall in projected state revenues resulted in a $24 million budget cut, however, and most institutions were hard pressed to handle an increase of 7.6 percent in cumulative enrollments of 173,212 students (1976 *Annual Report*).

In following years a School of Health Systems was established at Georgia Tech and a "three-two program" between Tech and Savannah State was initiated. The State's desegregation plan required a major overhaul in 1978, and the Board of Regents revised its policies for the Regents Test, Special Studies, and cut-off scores on the SAT. The changes in public demands and expectations are most evident, however, in the directions taken by the new Chancellor in 1979-1980. Southern Tech was established as a separate unit of the University System and major task forces were appointed to consider: (1) the optimal distribution of institutions within the State, (2) admission standards for the various units, (3) academic advising as a much needed service to students, and (4) affirmative action.

POLICIES AND ACADEMIC STANDARDS

Efforts to serve ever increasing numbers of students, many of whom were educationally disadvantaged, and increasing concerns for the maintenance of academic standards led to major revisions in Regents policies during the 1970s. After experimentation with summer admissions-on-trial programs and summer programs for enrichment and development, the Regents approved in 1973 the provision of Special Studies programs (later known as Developmental Studies) that would begin in September 1974. Early in 1972 a passing score on the "Rising Junior Test" was officially established as a graduation requirement for students earning degrees in institutions of the University System. And in 1979 the Regents gave official approval to the core curriculum for freshmen and sophomores that had been initiated in 1967.

The University System's response to the challenge of educationally disadvantaged students is evident in systemwide tests of reading and writing for "rising juniors" and developmental studies programs to assist students unable to meet regular admission standards. As one of the nation's first statewide systems to adopt standardized tests (i.e., the Scholastic Aptitude Test), the University System was quick to see the advantages of a systemwide test in basic skills for students moving from lower division coursework to upper division fields of specialization.

The policy decision to require such tests in all units of the University System was made in 1969. The stated purpose of such tests was to assure senior institutions that transferring students met explicit standards of academic competence. One implication of the requirement was to give stronger emphasis to the basic skills of reading and writing in lower division coursework, especially freshman English courses. In the beginning, however, a passing score was not required for graduation.

The failure rate of the Regents Test (as the test was later named) has been discouragingly high. One fourth of the students taking the test for the first time fail to make a passing score. The failure rate varied, of course, from institution to institution and occasionally ran as high as 85 percent for some institutions. Fortunately, students taking the test for a second time had a passing rate higher than those taking the test for the first time.

Later modifications were made in the Regents Testing Program as one component of its desegregation plan. In a 1984 agreement with the Office of Civil Rights, the Regents improved significantly the assistance given students who had failed the test. Students in the historically black institutions were required to complete approximately 50 instructional hours of remediation before retaking the test. Assistance to such students included sessions in which test-taking techniques were discussed *and* a student/teacher ratio of no more than twenty to one in remedial courses. In addition, the institutions developed reading and writing laboratories that were coordinated with remedial instruction. The coordination of such instruction with developmental and freshman English courses assured the Office of Civil Rights that students failing the Regents Test would benefit from programs of assistance more comparable to the services provided entering freshmen.

The establishment of programs of developmental studies in 1974 was directly related to the knowledge and experience gained in the Regents Testing Program. Regents policies specified that each institution would have a separate department or division of developmental studies, with a separate budget and staff. Funding for the program was to be on the same basis as other lower division programs of study. To tie the program firmly to the academic administration of each institution, Regents' policies further specified that the chairman of each developmental studies program would report directly to the chief academic officer of each institution "or his/her designee."

Other matters addressed in Regents policies for developmental studies were entrance requirements, exit requirements, and course credit. Originally set as a combined SAT score of less than 650 and confirming scores on the College Board's Comparative Guidance and Placement Test, entrance standards have been modified by separate cut-off scores for the verbal and mathematics sections of the SAT and by the development of a basic skills examination by members of the Regents' staff. In 1988 admission to developmental coursework was modified further through the use of a Comparative Placement Examination (CPE) that was developed by the American College Testing Program. To exit developmental courses, students must satisfy criteria decided by their respective institutions.

The courses taught in developmental studies were specified as English, reading, and writing but are not limited to such courses. Regents policies thereby encouraged the separate units to be responsive to the special needs of students in matters of personal, financial, academic, and career counseling. In addition, all institutions are required to provide academic advisement to ensure that students are informed about developmental requirements. No degree credit can be awarded for developmental coursework but institutional credit must be! Students thus can earn up to 30 hours of credit in developmental studies and all such credits are transferable to other University System institutions. The grading system used in developmental studies courses is identical with other academic grades within the institution.

Given its many years of experience with developmental studies the University System is, or should be, in a good position to assess the effectiveness of instruction in basic skills for educationally disadvantaged students. Roughly 19,000 students enroll in developmental studies each fall and for two-year colleges the enrollment averages about 25 percent of the institution's total enrollment. Senior college enrollments average about 12 percent of their total enrollment. The magnitude of the University System's effort is shown by estimates that one out of three students take some kind of remedial work in their freshman year. Programs are evaluated in terms of student retention, grades received in later coursework, completion of degree requirements, and other criteria involving comparison with regularly enrolled students.

When asked (in 1982) to judge the effectiveness of their programs, over 60 percent of the directors of developmental studies rated their programs as "moderately successful." At least one out of three directors rated their programs as "highly successful" while no director regarded his or her program as unsuccessful. The responding directors estimated that at least 53 percent of their students successfully exited developmental studies and that 36 percent completed a regular college program (Fincher, 1984).

GOVERNOR'S COMMITTEE ON POSTSECONDARY EDUCATION

The Educational Amendments Act of 1972 firmly endorsed statewide planning in its Section 1202 provisions for statewide planning commissions. Because of its confusion of "planning" with "planning and coordination," Section 1202 was not funded as quickly as other sections of the 1972 act, and the appointment of "1202 commissions" was delayed in most states. Georgia's first 1202 Commission, appointed by Governor Jimmy Carter, served quietly and with varying success for several years.

The decision to establish a separate public commission as the 1202 commission was advisable. Since Section 1202 provided for representation by four different sectors of postsecondary education—public higher education, private higher education, vocational-technical education, and proprietary education—there was an understandable reluctance on the part of the Board of Regents either to seek or to accept designation as Georgia's 1202 commission. For the same reason the State Board of Education could not be designated and a separate public commission was the only way in which to provide representation for the State's private and proprietary colleges.

In 1978 Governor George Busbee established a new 1202 commission with different and more specific responsibilities. To avoid confusion with the previous commission, he identified Georgia's 1202 agency as the Governor's Committee on Postsecondary Education and appointed David H. Gambrell, former U.S. Senator, as chairman. Other appointments to the committee were representative of the universities, senior colleges, and junior colleges in public higher education; universities and senior colleges in private higher education; public education at the elementary and secondary levels; the state's vocational-technical schools; proprietary education; and the state's business, industrial, and financial interests.

Governor Busbee defined the work of the committee as that of a problem-defining commission. He asked the group to "determine what the problems are, where our greatest needs lie, and what should be our priorities." The committee's response was given, one year later, in its report submitted to the governor. Entitled "Postsecondary Issues: Action Agenda for the Eighties," the report (COPE, 1979) defined ten major issues confronting postsecondary education in Georgia and suggested an agenda of ten statewide actions to be taken in resolving the defined issues. The issues themselves were stated in terms of statewide needs that concerned all sectors and levels of postsecondary education.

All sectors of postsecondary education were insufficiently recognized by the general public and better promotion of the state's diverse educational opportunities was needed. A comprehensive statement of postsecondary goals and improved communications (with better cooperation) among institutions was also needed. Issues should be identified before they become crises *and* an on-going process for identifying and analyzing issues should be established. The use of public resources should be more effective and efficient, and to this end the committee recommended better methods of assessing and reporting progress. A review of funding policies and processes was needed to ensure adequate funding and more effective budgeting. Taking note of widespread deficiencies in basic skills and the irrelevance (for later careers) of many postsecondary programs, the committee recommended a reconsideration of institutional responsibilities for teaching basic skills and a better balance in general and technical programs. To promote and to assure better cooperation among the four sectors of postsecondary education, an advisory commission for postsecondary education was suggested.

The State's need for a comprehensive statement of post-secondary goals and objectives was the issue delegated in 1979 to the second Governor's Committee on Postsecondary Education. Governor Busbee appointed himself chairman of the Second Governor's Committee and sought essentially the same representation of sectors and interests in the appointment of other members. The committee staff remained intact.

The statement of goals and objectives submitted the following year to the governor was indeed comprehensive. But like the issues defined earlier, the defined goals and objectives contained no surprises. Eight general goals were identified and grouped under the rubrics of individual development, diversity and accessibility, institutional responsiveness and excellence, effectiveness and efficiency in the use of public resources, and public awareness. Subsumed under the eight state-level goals were a varying number of objectives designed to tie the goals more tightly to specific policies, actions, and results.

- The intellectual, ethical, personal, and educational development of individuals to enable them to live in an effective, responsible, productive, and personally satisfying manner.

- Comprehensive, diversified, and accessible post-secondary education opportunities for the citizens of Georgia.

- Equitable opportunity for individuals to participate in postsecondary education, consistent with their abilities and needs, without regard to race, sex, age, religion, ethnic origin, economic status, or handicap.

- Responsiveness by postsecondary education to changing needs of individuals and society.

- Excellence in administration, instruction, research, and service consistent with institutional missions.

- The effective and efficient use of resources by public and private institutions in meeting institutional purposes.

- Communication and cooperation among educational institutions, associations and agencies related to postsecondary education, business, industry, labor, and government.

- Public awareness and knowledge of the availability, quality, and benefits offered by all sectors of postsecondary education.

Upon reappointment in 1980, the Governor's Committee began a series of studies to assess the progress that was being made toward state-level goals and objectives in postsecondary education. Neither the Governor nor the committee had set goals and objectives for institutions, programs, or professional personnel. The committee had merely defined in one document the stated or implied goals of existing institutions or programs. The committee's work then became one of assessing the progress postsecondary institutions and programs were making toward those goals.

The Governor's Committee again rendered valuable service in its third year as a 1202 commission. The assessment of progress proceeded in various ways. Six doctoral students in higher education at the University of Georgia contributed doctoral dissertations to the committee's work. The dissertations were statewide surveys of interinstitutional cooperation, community services, honors programs for superior students, advanced placement and course exemption policies, student retention, and the reactions of corporate recruiters to college graduates from Georgia institutions. A seventh survey, not developed as a doctoral dissertation, dealt with student services.

In 1981 the Governor's Committee submitted its third report and, perhaps for the first time, conveyed the remarkable diversity of private and public postsecondary education in Georgia. An institutional inventory disclosed at least 308 institutions providing some form of education beyond the high school and worthy of the name postsecondary education. Within the state were: 34 public colleges or universities; 40 private colleges or universities; 30 public vocational-technical schools; 10 private certificate or diploma schools; and 206 proprietary schools, 10 of which were degree-granting.

Progress was clearly evident in the diversity of opportunities, but public awareness of postsecondary opportunities was another matter. The committee recommended a directory, inclusive of all postsecondary programs, and later published such a directory in tabloid form under the title of *The Bridge*. The publication of this directory continued in 1983 when a third edition was released by Governor Joe Frank Harris.

The committee, concluding from its various studies that the future of private education in Georgia was relatively secure, recommended that state assistance to students in private colleges remain at its relative level to per-student allocations in public institutions. Postsecondary institutions evidently were meeting the career needs of students but there were reservations about their responsiveness to changing demands. Academic, career, and personal counseling services were not readily available to many students and institutions were lax in meeting the demand for noncredit, part-time, special/remedial, nontraditional forms of instruction and training. Student financial aid was still inadequate, with too large a portion of it being federal funds only.

In December 1982 the Governor's Committee, continuing its work without federal funds, issued a report summarizing its work for the previous four years and recommending priorities in postsecondary education for the future (COPE, 1982). Addressing again the issue of student financial aid to private accredited institutions, the committee recommended the conversion of the State's Tuition Equalization Grant program to a needs-based program. Restated were its earlier recommendations of funding relative to University System per-student allocations and the inclusion of appropriately accredited proprietary schools. Added was a recommended proviso that financial aid should go only to students "able to benefit from postsecondary education."

Anticipating the work of several national commissions, the committee recommended that postsecondary institutions "clearly define their expectations of high school prerequisites . . . and assist high schools in meeting those expectations." Also recommended were more definite admission requirements for colleges. These requirements should be consistent with student abilities, as measured by standardized ability and achievement tests and previous academic performance. With respect to instruction in basic skills, the committee recommended that no degree, certificate, or diploma credit be given for such instruction and called upon colleges for "policy plans" that would eventually phase out all developmental studies programs.

Future concerns for postsecondary education in Georgia included: (a) the coordination of secondary and postsecondary efforts in the development of basic skills; (b) the low rate of participation in postsecondary education by Georgia residents; (c) the adequacy of student financial aid; (d) the improvement of funding and budgeting; (e) the governance of vocational-technical education; and (f) clearer definitions of institutional roles. The concluding section of the 1982 report again stated the public need for an advisory commission on postsecondary education with statutory authority.

Although the Governor's Committee was officially continued by Governor Harris until July 1983, the committee did not meet again and its fourth major report was its final report. The committee staff continued as an office under the new administration but consisted in 1984 of only the director and a senior planner.

REGENTS DESEGREGATION PLAN

In 1978 the Regents extensively revised their plan for desegregation by addressing more directly the elimination of duplication in business administration and teacher education programs at

Savannah State and Armstrong State colleges. Operating under federal guidelines that fostered the preservation of institutional identity while removing vestiges of dualism, the Regents transferred to Armstrong State all undergraduate and graduate courses in teacher education at Savannah State. In similar manner they transferred to Savannah State all undergraduate and graduate programs in business administration at Armstrong State. Faculty members involved in the transferred programs were reassigned to the other institution. As part of the plan, the stipulation was made that appropriations for the two colleges would not be affected as a result of enrollment fluctuations.

The Regents plan was adopted at a time when similar considerations were underway in the cities of Nashville and Norfolk. The plan for Savannah differed, however, from the decisions made in the other areas by being the explicit plan of a governing board responsible for both institutions. In Nashville the merger of two somewhat similar institutions was ordered by a federal court, and in Norfolk joint planning for inter-institutional co-operation was mandated by state and federal officials.

In the first year of the implemented plan, enrollments declined at both Armstrong State and Savannah State. Other-race presence on the two campuses was noticeably increased by virtue of the conditions under which presently enrolled students could transfer. In both institutions students maintained an option of graduating with degrees conferred by the institution from which they had transferred. Other conditions of transfer assured that academic credit would not be lost and completion of degree programs would not be delayed. During the second year slight gains in total enrollments occurred at both institutions, but total gains were accompanied by slight declines in other-race enrollments.

The effectiveness of program transfer as a means of deseg-regation was not evident ten years later when an intensive consolidation study was conducted. Total enrollments at both institutions had declined from 1978 through 1987. In business administration programs the enrollment at Savannah State was significantly less than the combined enrollment at the two institutions ten year earlier. At Armstrong State an increase was observed for the total enrollments in teacher education, but the number of teacher education students who were black had decreased.

The success of the Regents' plan was more evident in the establishment of a joint continuing education program that was housed in downtown Savannah. The Coastal Georgia Center for Continuing Education now has its own conference facilities, benefits from an unusually favorable location in the historic district of Savannah, and continues to be jointly staffed by the two institutions.

Other features of the Regents' desegregation plan included an inter-campus unit for the administration of all joint efforts between Albany State and Albany Junior colleges, a "two-plus-two" academic program for the same two institutions, a criminal justice institute at Albany State, and other programs involving student incentives and distinguished scholars. The plan received "formal unconditional approval" by the Office of Civil Rights in March 1979.

PLANNING IN THE 1980s

In the early 1980s the Board of Regents addressed several major policy issues dealing with finance, the future of public higher education in the State, the potential uses of telecommunications in University System programs and services, the State's need for programs in the health professions, off-campus degree programs, and statewide assessment in nursing education. The University System of Georgia was re-affirmed as a statewide system of public higher education; the organization and function of its separate institutions were to be reviewed; methods of funding and financing were to be proposed; and continued growth and development were to be based on systematic inquiry and analysis.

STUDY COMMITTEE ON FINANCE

In January 1981 the Board of Regents, the General Assembly, and the Governor jointly appointed a Study Committee on Public Higher Education Finance. Appointments to the study committee were representative of the three sponsoring agencies, private higher education, and the state's business and professional interests. Staff work for the Committee was provided by an independent, out-of-state consulting agency. The study committee adopted as guiding principles to its work: (a) the need to continue improvement of the quality of the University System; (b) the need for more efficient management; and (c) the need for a funding system that would provide incentives for quality improvement and efficient management. A more basic premise on which the committee began its work was the inadequacy of the funding formula that originated with the 1963 Governor's Commission To Improve Education.

The findings and recommendations of the study committee were presented in September 1982 by Governor Busbee to "All Georgians Interested in Higher Education." The major recommendations called for a more equitable sharing of educational costs and specified that student tuition should account for 25 percent of total revenue for general operations in the resident instruction budget. To attain this proportionate sharing of costs, tuition should be increased 15 percent annually until the 25 percent objective was reached.

To foster efficient management of institutional resources, the study committee recommended that institutions be permitted to carry forward unexpended funds for one year and use such funds for nonrecurring items such as equipment and library materials. Also recommended for the purpose of efficient management was the retention of 85 percent of indirect cost recoveries on sponsored research and other externally funded programs.

The funding formula recommended by the study committee specified major categories for: (a) instruction and research,

(b) public service, (c) academic support, (d) student services and institutional support, and (e) plant operation and maintenance. For instruction and research, the committee recommended funding by lower division, upper division, and graduate levels and by five instructional or programs areas—corresponding roughly to behavioral and social sciences; professional and applied fields; arts, sciences, and foreign languages; developmental education; and medicine, dentistry, and veterinary medicine.

Other details of the formula specified academic support at 17.7 percent of the funding base established for instruction, research, and public service; student services and institutional support at 23.1 percent of that funding base; and a special provision for quality improvement at one percent of the total budget. The proposed funding system would maintain Georgia's rank among the upper fourth of southern states and focus attention on strategies for quality improvement. No provisions were made in the formula for protecting institutions from declining enrollments and where enrollments did decline, the Regents were encouraged to examine carefully the continued need for those institutions.

The recommendations of the Study Committee on Public Higher Education Finance thus had many promising implications for the improvement of education. The quality improvement provision would create funds for faculty recruitment and retention, professional development programs for faculty, the development of special programs, and the purchase of special classroom and laboratory equipment.

STATEWIDE NEEDS ASSESSMENT

In August 1981 the Board of Regents initiated "a comprehensive statewide needs assessment designed to provide a foundation for charting the course for public higher education in the state." The resulting report, "The Eighties and Beyond: A Commitment to Excellence," was the most relevant statement on public higher education in Georgia since the report of the 1963 Governor's Commission To Improve Education. The statewide needs assessment was conducted within the span of one year and was rightly expected to provide a basis for planning and development within the University System. The objectives of the Regents study were: (1) to analyze current programs of instruction, research, and service—and to identify additional services that should be provided; (2) to determine if the present complex of institutions is sufficient for meeting identified needs; and (3) to project changes that will be necessary in the foreseeable future.

Noting that the success of the University System in the 1960s and 1970s was judged in terms of growth, the needs assessment report declared the improvement of educational quality to be the measure of success in the 1980s. The first recommendation in the report called for establishment by the Governor, General Assembly, and Board of Regents of quality improvement as the top priority for public higher education. The report endorsed the study committee on finance's report as "one of the most significant documents in the history of the University System" and recommended its full implementation (p. 19). The introduction to the report referred to the study committee on finance's report as a significant companion document.

Having declared quality improvement as its top priority, the coordinating committee for the study recommended: (a) closer cooperation between the Regents and the State Board of Education; (b) creative partnerships with community, business, and industrial leaders; (c) a system of program evaluation with both internal and external efforts; (d) a long-range goal of eliminating developmental studies; (e) the reinstitution of specific academic requirements for admission to units of the University System; and (f) a systemwide program of faculty development.

Concerning the structure or institutional composition of the University System, the coordinating committee recommended that no changes be made in present institutional structure or status. Existing institutions were to be carefully monitored, however, to determine if declining enrollments implied closing or consolidation. In the meantime, better use was to be made of cooperative residential doctoral programs, telecommunications, and satellite research centers to deliver needed services. The Board of Regents was expected to study its institutions in Albany and Savannah and to determine if their present structure served the needs of their respective areas and the state as a whole.

A major strength of the University System was identified as its governing structure and the leadership it could provide. The Regents, therefore, were to set priorities for institutional and program development and to make those priorities known. They were to take a more direct hand in the definition of institutional missions and ensure that institutional missions supported the University System as a whole. The Board would continue to delegate to institutions the autonomy they required for diversity and academic excellence, but the Board should readdress the problem of institutional service areas and refine its guidelines so as not to encourage unhealthy competition.

Other recommendations to the Board of Regents included: (a) strengthening the periodic review of institutional productivity and management; (b) studying institutional and program duplication with an eye to consolidation; and (c) measuring institutional productivity in terms of academic excellence, as well as the usual quantitative indices. In accomplishing these recommendations the Board should also strive for better communications with both the citizens of Georgia and their elected representatives in the General Assembly.

Recommendations concerning institutional and/or program matters were directed to: (1) the liberal and fine arts, as the core of instruction in each of the units; (2) agriculture, as a highly specialized and scientifically oriented industry; (3) business, industry, and technology, as significant partners in the creation of economic wealth and well-being; (4) the medical and health professions, as a cluster of particularly important service occupations; (5) teacher education, as a profession requiring close study; (6) research, as a function requiring continuing overall commitment as an essential part of the University System's mission; (7) public service and continuing education, as functions and responsibilities with increasing importance, and (8) public and social services, as areas of community need that are subject to change.

The Regents Needs Assessment Report closed with a cogent statement of the University System's role and functions as "a cohesive and coordinated response to the public higher education needs of the state" and a nod in the direction of its next fifty years of service. Reaffirmed was its commitment to the "basic operating principle articulated by the first Board in 1932—the responsibility to determine what will best serve the educational interests of the state as a whole."

OTHER SYSTEMWIDE STUDIES

The advent of the adult learner and other nontraditional students was an unheralded blessing on many college campuses nationally and within the State of Georgia. In many uncalibrated ways the increased demand for higher education by older students, new students, and part-time students was the salvation of many colleges during the 1970s and the 1980s. During the 1980s alone the traditional college-age population (18-24 years) of the nation declined 15 percent while the population of adults (25-44 years) increased by 20 percent.

As a systemwide study in 1983 disclosed, adult learners within the University System averaged 31 years in age and almost one-half of the group was 30 years of age or younger. This finding suggested that adult learners in Georgia's public colleges were not so much adult learners as they were returning students or late-starters. Almost two out of three of the group were women, and an overwhelming majority were white.

The secondary preparation of adult learners in the study compared favorably with that of many other "traditional students" within the University System. The high school average of the adult learners was a substantial "C" average, but a larger proportion of the group had high school grades below average.

With respect to their performance on the SAT, adult learners scored appreciably lower but not in ways that were unexpected. As a group, they scored at a creditable level on the verbal section of the SAT and at a lower level on the mathematics section. More noticeable differences were observed in the higher verbal scores of women and the higher mathematics scores of men. The same differences were observed in a subgroup who had not completed high school. Despite the discontinuance of their secondary schooling at an early age, the adult learners in the study scored acceptably well on a standardized test of academic ability and met, with reasonable satisfaction, the course requirements and faculty expectations of institutions within the System.

Classroom performance, as reflected in freshman grades, was related to the adult learners' reasons for continuing their education, the type of program in which they enrolled, and the level of the institution in which they were enrolled. A major finding of the study indicates that adult learners, like many transfer students, may experience difficulty during their first quarter of enrollment but their academic performance improves significantly with classroom experience (Fincher, 1983).

Another systemwide survey in 1986 found that the admissions data presented in the annual norms booklets is often used in unpublicized ways by administrators, faculty, and staff who are involved in academic decision making. Most relevant, perhaps, is the finding that the admissions data collected annually have many uses not directly related to admission decisions. High school counselors are among the most frequent users of SAT scores in helping high school students identify colleges to which they might apply. After admissions, test scores and high school grades may be used for academic awards or other forms of student recognition prior to the earning of freshman grades. In all cases, however, the uses of such information is always in conjunction with other information that has been gathered on students.

Other effective uses of the SAT were found in academic placement, class sectioning, academic advising, personal counseling, and in institutional research and planning. SAT scores do not appear to be used widely, however, in the evaluation or assessment of academic programs. The predictive efficiency of the SAT has been the subject of several doctoral dissertations within the State's universities. All such studies reflect the SAT's usefulness and effectiveness in predicting grades but suggest that the SAT's major value is the information it provides about student abilities and achievement. (Fincher, 1986).

POLICY DECISIONS IN 1980-1984

In the early 1980s many challenging policy decisions were placed on the Board of Regents' agenda. Policy changes requiring attention were recurrent issues, such as changes in institutional status and the geographical distribution of educational opportunity in graduate education. Other major decisions were needed in areas of policy related to the State's commitment to academic excellence *and* to equity or fairness for the University System's changing constituencies. The size and complexity of 34 diverse institutions educating over 120,000 students challenged the governance capabilities of the Board of Regents, as well as the administrative competence of institutional leaders.

The approval of new degree programs and the authorization of inter-institutional programs that would extend opportunities for graduate education—without encouraging (unduly) institutional aspirations for enhanced status—required a substantial amount of time and effort. Procedures and guidelines for cooperative programs were approved in 1980, and opportunities for participation in doctoral programs were extended to senior colleges working in cooperation with the University of Georgia and Georgia State University. In similar manner, cooperation between units of the University System and institutions outside the System were encouraged under policies permitting the establishment of joint programs. Programs in the health professions continued to expand and to require new forms of cooperative agreements with clinical agencies and organizations.

In December 1980 the Board adopted a policy statement concerning procedures for determining the feasibility of changes in institutional mission and status. Three colleges were seeking university status, and a fourth was seeking elevation to the level of senior college. Other policy changes of major importance concerned: (a) faculty salaries for entry-level positions, (b) the dismissal, demotion, or suspension of classified personnel, (c) the provision of grievance procedures, and (d) revision of employee benefits, such as insurance. During 1981-1982 the Regents successfully defended their constitutional authority in the State's revision of its 1945 Constitution. Another policy decision made at that time gave institutions an option in admitting students who had not previously attended college and who had been out of high school for at least eight years. Other policy statements adopted by the Board of Regents in the early 1980s dealt with academic advisement and with basic requirements for the University System's core curriculum.

In January 1981 the Regents adopted the recommendation of the Georgia Public Telecommunications Task Force that the System's public television station be placed under the authority of a newly created Public Telecommunications Commission. One of the reasons given for the Regents' decision was the "opportunity" to work more closely with the State Board and State Department of Education.

Following a recommendation of its Task Force on Optimal Distribution of Institutions, the Board adopted a more "functional classification" of institutions in which: universities were classified as either Comprehensive (Category A) or Special Purpose (Category B); senior colleges were classified as either Senior College (A) or Special Purpose (B), and junior colleges were Category A (offering transfer and career programs) or Category B (offering transfer, career, *and* vocational-technical programs).

In 1983 the Regents adopted a revised policy manual in which efforts were made to eliminate inconsistencies and to reflect more accurately the numerous changes made in systemwide policies. Among the new policies included in the revised manual were: (1) provisions for external degree programs, (2) changes in the academic calendar for the University of Georgia law school, (3) revisions in policies concerning developmental studies, and (4) revisions in the University System's tenure and nontenure policies.

Policy issues on the Regents' agenda in 1983-1984 were: (1) college participation rates and ways in which institutions could increase participation, (2) ways in which DeKalb Community College could become a unit of the University System, (3) agreements with the State Board of Education that would implement Governor Joe Frank Harris' establishment of "a third board" for Postsecondary Vocational-Technical Education, (4) adoption of a pre-college curriculum requirement for admission to the University System, and (5) evidence of "substantial progress" in meeting the State's desegregation goals. Initiated during the year was a formal procedure for the review and improvement of teacher education programs not having a 70 percent passing rate on the State's Teacher Certification Test (TCT).

In the same year a study of engineering education by the staff of the Southern Regional Education Board was contracted, and approval to become a four-year institution was given to Clayton Junior College. Approval was also given "provisional admission criteria" that would apply to freshmen not meeting the requirements of the Regents' 1988 pre-college curriculum. And as in many previous years, the Regents sought ways in which better lines of communication could be established with the State's private institutions.

In summary, the University System in the early 1980s reached a level of notable maturity. Its fiftieth anniversary was quietly observed and passed unnoticed by the news media and the great majority of its constituents. Thirty-three institutions of higher education served well the needs of Georgians for undergraduate, graduate, and professional education. The unspoken goals of self-sufficiency and respectability had long been met, and plans for geographical distribution had been implemented well. The respective institutions and their faculties were in quest of national recognition and noticeable progress was evident in many institutional commitments to excellence. The diversification of institutions and programs was an acceptable, if not complete, match for the pluralistic needs and preferences of the System's constituencies. Progress had been made in minority access and equity, women were the majority students in many classes and in some institutions, and adult learners were enrolled throughout the System. Certain problems did persist, however, as 40 percent or more of the University System's entering freshmen scored in the lower third of the nation's high school graduates in basic skills of literacy. Far too many could not read, write, or reason as well as previous generations of college students. And despite the effectiveness of developmental studies, too many graduates left the classrooms of colleges and universities with lingering deficiencies in basic academic competencies.

With the 1980s came new challenges, demands, expectations, and needs. As the separate institutions coped with changing demands and expectations, their success was varied and uneven. The momentum gained in twenty years of rapid growth and expansion was commendable but difficult to sustain. Once again, the University System was called upon to lend its institutions, programs, and talents to the solution of societal problems and the resolution of complex issues in public policy. The Board of Regents' agenda was increasingly crowded with matters of national and regional urgency, as well as the internal rivalries of ambitious and energetic institutions.

CHAPTER SIX

Review and Coordination: 1984-1990

If we learn from the past but are not captive to it, we are more likely to have the ability to build a vision for the future that, when realized, will lead to making right those things that are wrong, making better those things that are good.
Chancellor H. Dean Propst, *System Summary,* 1990

Beginning in 1985-1986 the University System obtained, for the first time, full funding of the revised "formula for excellence" recommended by the 1982 Study Committee on Public Higher Education Finance. The new chancellor noted in his annual report "the constructive working relations that have been forged between the Board of Regents and the Board for Postsecondary Vocational Education." The report submitted by the Southern Regional Education Board did *not* support the State's need for a second engineering school and, to the contrary, presented evidence that Georgia Tech was not adequately supported in providing engineering programs that had long served state and national needs.

The status of the University System in 1986 was evident in an equivalent-full-time enrollment of 113,685 students and a total enrollment of 135,964 students. A total of 24,040 degrees and certificates was conferred, and at least 6,199 faculty members, making an average salary of $31,039, were involved in teaching, research, and service. Over 12,550 continuing education programs had a total of 472,730 participants.

The institutional composition of the University System was again changed in 1986 when DeKalb Community College became the 34th unit. Since 1964 DeKalb Community College had been the only junior college established under the Junior College Act of 1958 and the only public institution of higher education that was *not* under the jurisdiction of the Board of Regents. In the same year Clayton Junior College was advanced to senior college status and re-named Clayton State. In many respects the changing status of the two colleges brought to completion a network of institutions in the Atlanta area that was discussed in 1964 by the Regents Study Committee on Community Junior Colleges.

Further changes in the System's composition followed in 1988 when the State's junior colleges were permitted to drop the word "junior" and select a title more in keeping with their varied missions. As part of a general effort to facilitate the effectiveness of two-year colleges in meeting community needs, the Chancellor had appointed in 1987 a study committee, chaired by President Derrell C. Roberts of Dalton Junior College, to make recommendations concerning the mission and roles of Georgia's public two-year colleges. The committee concluded from its study that mission statements should re-affirm the public two-year colleges as "an essential part of Georgia's statewide system of public higher education," and expand the means and locations by which students earn degrees. Five major roles for two-year colleges were defined as the provision of: (1) general education, (2) lower division coursework that would transfer to senior colleges, (3) instructional and developmental courses for inadequately prepared students, (4) career-related programs that required college-level instruction, and (5) service programs and activities for their respective communities.

Respondents to the committee's survey were confident that two-year colleges could provide high quality transfer programs and yet be comprehensive in the programs and services they offered. Despite funding differences between the two, academic programs of instruction and continuing education programs were regarded as fully compatible. Respondents were unanimous in their belief that the differences between two-year colleges and other postsecondary institutions should be emphasized and more adequately publicized.

Survey findings and committee recommendations were submitted to the Board of Regents in November 1986. In addition to the changes in institutional names, the Board of Regents

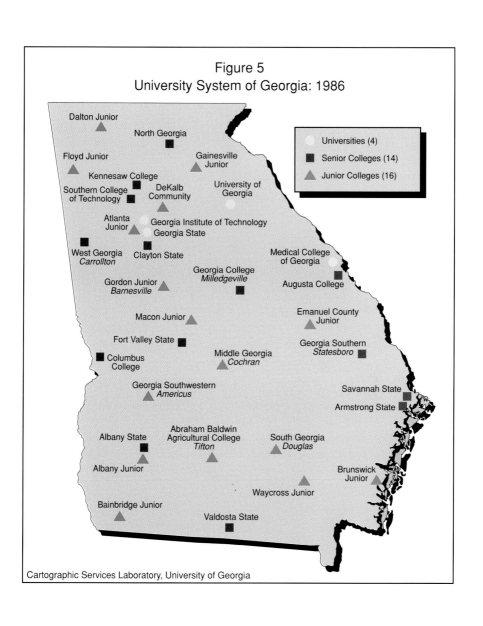

Figure 5
University System of Georgia: 1986

Universities (4)
Senior Colleges (14)
Junior Colleges (16)

Dalton Junior
North Georgia
Floyd Junior
Gainesville Junior
Kennesaw College
Southern College of Technology
DeKalb Community
University of Georgia
Atlanta Junior
Georgia Institute of Technology
Georgia State
West Georgia Carrollton
Clayton State
Medical College of Georgia
Gordon Junior Barnesville
Georgia College Milledgeville
Augusta College
Macon Junior
Emanuel County Junior
Fort Valley State
Columbus College
Middle Georgia Cochran
Georgia Southern Statesboro
Georgia Southwestern Americus
Savannah State
Armstrong State
Albany State
Abraham Baldwin Agricultural College Tifton
South Georgia Douglas
Albany Junior
Brunswick Junior
Bainbridge Junior
Waycross Junior
Valdosta State

Cartographic Services Laboratory, University of Georgia

approved at a subsequent meeting differential admission standards that would permit the colleges to distinguish between applicants seeking vocational or technical training and academic coursework for transfer to a four-year institution.

ASSESSMENT AND ACCOUNTABILITY

Policy and program decisions in the late 1980s were increasingly concerned with institutional effectiveness and accountability in meeting the changing demands and expectations of the University System's constituencies. The assessment of academic programs had been a policy issue throughout the 1970s. Federal legislation and regulations gave an impetus to program evaluation and other funding agencies had followed their lead. In 1977 a subcommittee of the Administrative Advisory Council had been appointed to study ways in which the assessment of academic degree programs could be facilitated within the University System. A survey by the subcommittee revealed considerable readiness within the System to assess and to evaluate academic programs, but a decided preference for local norms and internal standards was expressed by most respondents. Appreciable consensus was found in the need of institutions for methods of program assessment that would help determine the direction of future program development.

The subcommittee, accepting the survey findings as the basis for its work, directed its further efforts to the development of a rationale whereby program assessment within the separate institutions would lead to the improvement of undergraduate instruction while maintaining institutional autonomy or independence in deciding program content and academic standards. In its report the subcommittee clearly stated the difficulties of program assessment in a statewide system as varied as the University System of Georgia. Neither program objectives nor outcomes could be uniform *at* university, senior college, and junior college levels and *across* the diverse academic departments of the different institutions.

The subcommittee report recommended options and alternatives whereby departments of instruction would accept responsibility for the assessment of all programs in which departmental staffs decided course objectives and requirements. To meet its responsibilities in assessment, each department should define the program to be assessed, specify the methods of assessment used, and report all findings and conclusions to academic officials. A definite option open to each department was the selection, adaptation, or construction of assessment instruments that would serve their particular purposes. Among the many alternatives suggested to departments were formal or traditional methods such as standardized tests, semi-formal or structured techniques such as the use of outside examiners and simulation exercises, and informal means such as internships, apprenticeships, etc.

The subcommittee's intent in developing a rationale and suggesting departmental options was to engage the academic departments themselves in the active assessment and evaluation of learning outcomes. The reactions of several departments, however, was to the contrary. Many faculty members saw the assessment of student learning (by means other than course grades) as an evaluation of teaching effectiveness. As the result of faculty resistance and other conditions at the time, exit examinations were unevenly applied as a means of program assessment and as evidence of institutional accountability.

Among the conditions fostering accountability in the 1980s was a returning concern with inter-institutional cooperation and working agreements with other state agencies having responsibilities in the various sectors of postsecondary education. In cooperation with the State Board of Education, the Regents established higher admission standards for students entering units of the University System. For applicants planning to enroll in degree programs (leading to a baccalaureate), four units of high school English, three units of science, and three units of mathematics would be required in the fall of 1988 and thereafter. Also included in the requirements were three units in social science and two units in a foreign language. As admission requirements, the courses were regarded as minimum standards for successful performance at the college level. As customary in establishing systemwide policies, all units of the University System retained the right to set higher standards.

In raising admission standards for the entire System the Regents were influenced significantly by the College Board's definition of basic academic competencies that are needed in virtually all areas of college coursework. To publicize its new admission standards the Regents published an attractive brochure in which the "essential courses and skills" were identified and discussed in terms of their relevance for educational achievement. Following the first year of implementation, a doctoral dissertation (Albright, 1990) found that completion of the college preparatory curriculum in high school was indeed predictive of academic success at the college freshman level. When other factors such as SAT scores and high school averages were controlled, the effect was small but nonetheless statistically significant *and* promising.

Other forms of cooperation were involved in the creation of the Board of Adult and Technical Education. Established first by executive order as a board of postsecondary education and later receiving statutory status under the Quality Basic Education Act of 1985, the new state board sought ways in which associate degrees could be offered in the State's technical schools. The potential for conflict was obvious in the career programs of junior colleges and the need for fundamental or general education courses in the associate degree programs of technical schools. Cooperative agreements between the two boards thus was essential to the effective operations of their respective institutions. In many ways the situation was reminiscent of the conditions studied by the Governor's Commission To Improve Education in the early 1960s.

Educational and training programs for the health professions was another area in which conditions were reminiscent of earlier years. In 1985 the Georgia Student Finance Authority funded an extensive needs assessment study of over twenty-five health professions within the State. Documented in that study were severe shortages of personnel in nursing, occupational therapy, and physical therapy. Less severe shortages were found in other allied fields such as radiological technology and the laboratory sciences. The supply of educated and trained personnel was not sufficient to meet the demands of health care institutions. Nursing, in particular, was a profession requiring special attention from the Regents Committee on Health Education (Morris, 1987). Once again, the recurrent concern for the education of health professions personnel dealt with limited supply and increasing demands in health and medical care.

REGENTS ADMINISTRATIVE DEVELOPMENT PROGRAM

An important feature of the 1984 revision of the Regents desegregation plan was the provision of an administrative development program for minority faculty members. The program began in the fall of 1984 and continued for three years until 1987. Under the conditions of participation in the program, faculty members within units of the University System were nominated by their presidents and selected after an extensive interview with members of the Chancellor's staff. The interview served both to inform the nominees about the objectives and procedures of the program and to assess their readiness for an intensive program involving seminars, workshops, and internships over a nine-months period.

Selected participants began their internship by attending a two-week seminar conducted at the Georgia Center for Continuing Education in Athens. The seminar was taught by the staff of the Institute of Higher Education and an option for participants was two hours of graduate credit as inservice education. The substance and content of the two-week seminar was an overview of higher education in the nation and state, an indepth look at the University System of Georgia and its various institutions and programs, and an intensive discussion of administrative concepts and principles. Following the seminar the Regents Fellows reported to the supervising administrator with whom they worked during the academic year. By observing, studying, and participating in administrative decisions, the Regents Fellows were exposed to administrative duties and responsibilities in an unusually effective manner. They were also exposed to University System policy decisions by attending a meeting of the Board of Regents and (with their host president) a meeting of the University System Advisory Committee. Interviews with the Chancellor and his staff were also scheduled for each participant, as part of his or her observation and study of the University System.

In the winter quarter the Regents Fellows returned to Athens for a two-day workshop with experienced academic administrators. In the spring they closed out the year with an intensive, week-long evaluation workshop in which they reviewed with their colleagues their activities and experiences. At the end of the workshop each participant evaluated the overall program, including the formal and informal aspects of the year's activities.

The effectiveness of the Regents Administrative Development Program has been assessed in a doctoral dissertation written concurrently with the program (Booth, 1987). Twenty-six faculty members participated in the program and at least nine of them were involved in a significantly higher level of administration a year after completing their fellowship. Other participants benefitted from the program in other ways, and none regarded the program as a waste of public or personal resources. Individual benefits were matched by various benefits to the institutions at which the Regents Fellows served. The extent of participation is further indication of the program's effectiveness. Over twenty different units of the University System participated in the program as either a home or host institution.

In 1987-1988 the Regents Administrative Development Program was extended for a year in a provisional effort to assist recently appointed administrators within the University System. Presidents were asked to nominate deans, directors, or department heads who had recently assumed administrative responsibilities and who would be interested in participating in a developmental workshop prior to the opening of the fall term. Nominating institutions were responsible for the travel expenses of participants and for such support as they might be able to give a developmental project that each participant would conduct during the year. The Institute of Higher Education was responsible for the opening workshop in the fall and for a closing workshop in the spring.

The quick response to the Chancellor's request for nominations resulted in two fall workshops, one in August and another in September after several administrators had assumed new duties. Each fall workshop was similar in format and substance to those conducted for Regents Administrative Fellows. At the spring workshop in 1988, twelve of the fall participants presented papers that had been organized and written during the past year.

AN ASSESSMENT OF THE SYSTEM

In 1987 President Noah Langdale of Georgia State University was asked by the Chancellor to undertake an indepth assessment of the University System, its current status, and its prospects for the future. Included in the Chancellor's list of charges were 25 issues, problems, and concerns that were within the purview of the Regents' control and authority. The study was concluded two years later and presented to the Board of Regents on December 13, 1989.

The scope of the assessment study was a "retrospective and prospective examination" of the University System. The rationale by which the study proceeded was the coalescence of President Langdale's experience as president for thirty years with the related experiences of other well informed, actively involved participants in the University System's growth and development since the 1950s. Working with President Langdale were W. Lee Burge, former chairman of the Board of Regents; John W. Hooper, former vice chancellor of the University System; and Cameron Fincher, director of the Institute of Higher Education. Assisting in the study were the presidents of the 34 units and numerous vice presidents, deans, directors, or department heads who submitted reports on the diverse institutional functions under their supervision.

In its coverage of varied and complex issues, the assessment report conveys the scope and the complexity of the problems with which institutional leaders in public higher education must cope. Policies, programs, and problems were considered as part of more complex, more significant events taking place at national, regional, and state levels. By presenting historical, national, and regional perspectives, the report brought out many distinctive features of Georgia's system of higher education and identified many common policy issues which all institutions and statewide systems must effectively resolve.

The report discusses a dozen or more driving forces that facilitate or impede the progress of the University System. Among these forces is the "ageing" of the System's institutions, facilities, faculties, programs, and services. Having succeeded in its many efforts to fulfill educational needs and public expectations, the University System became, in many respects, "a victim of its own success" with new and different competitors for public resources. As demands for educational services increase, the University System will be strongly challenged to renew and to enhance its resources and capabilities. Other driving forces are national purposes and objectives, as seen in the influence of public policy and federal legislation; continued access and equity for minority groups, as seen in the national push for integration and equality; and a returning concern for "the basics, classics, and ethics" as institutions in the University System cope with the increasing cultural diversity of their students. Accompanying (and often countering) these forces are public indifference, technological obsolescence, over extended specialization, widespread tendencies to trivialize, and a failure to honor (in education) what we seek to promote.

In meeting its challenges of the past the University System has contributed to various paradoxes that must be resolved more effectively. In many functions and activities of our colleges and universities, there is far more data collected and distributed than information or knowledge. Within our institutions there is more emphasis on pragmatic results than the liberal arts. In teaching and instruction there is often more concern with "partial success" and "extrinsic rewards" than excellence and personal satisfaction. And in fulfilling institutional responsibilities, more attention is given to "cost-cutting" efficiencies than to the development and appreciation of human competence or proficiency.

An unusually valuable contribution to the report was made by the presidents of University System institutions. In responding to the policy issues with which the assessment was concerned, presidents of the various units provided insights and perspectives that must be considered in the future development of the University System. As a group, they were seriously concerned about public perceptions of higher education and the "erosion" of public confidence in the quality and relative value of college instruction. They were aware of declining academic standards but believed that the State's leaders in higher education can address the issue satisfactorily. They were in agreement that "non-applicable studies" can be eliminated from college curricula, but they did not expect developmental studies to be eliminated in the foreseeable future. The declining pool of high school graduates will have an adverse effect on higher education, and efforts must be made to reduce dropouts in secondary education. In matters of staffing and organization, they were not worried about student/faculty ratios, "surplus educational capacity," administrative staff replacements, or federal regulations; they were worried about acute faculty shortages in selected academic disciplines. Thus, they regarded faculty salaries as "perhaps the most serious need" in the University System, and they would like to see "more flexibility" in administrative salaries to permit recognition of merit. In the maintenance and replacement of physical facilities and instructional equipment, presidents did not regard "present funding mechanisms" as adequate. Inflationary library costs are "a dilemma" and preclude the most effective use of library resources. In their recruitment, enrollment, and employment of minorities, the presidents expressed disappointment. They expressed further disappointment in their retention of minorities after successful recruitment.

The assessment report concluded with a detailed discussion of the observations made during the assessment study. Included in the observations are numerous suggestions for consideration by the Chancellor and the Board of Regents. Explicit in the assessment report is the need for a statewide commitment to higher education that involves the cooperation of state government. Such a commitment is dependent upon the creation of "a climate of urgency" and the assistance of institutional constituencies in making a unified effort to support higher education. If the University System's financial needs are to be met, past budgeting practices, such as enrollment-driven formulas, will not suffice and "extraordinary funding" will be necessary.

Higher education, the report notes, is often criticized for its "order-taking" attitude and for its inclination to measure "what can be measured." The former leads to indifference in institutions of higher education and the latter leads to the corollary that "what cannot be measured" is unimportant. In the assessment study, no "posture for change" was readily found, and when educational reform became a topic for consideration there is a tendency to seek either simplistic or totalistic solutions. Yet, assessment and accountability are "dominating terms" in higher education and institutions must answer national criticisms. The report takes special notice of the challenge to public higher education by the "privatization" of government functions and by private schools that are profit-driven.

The Board of Regents was urged to take a stronger interest in undergraduate education and its improvement. Over compartmentalization of the curriculum and its resulting trivialization of academic subject matter should be avoided. Whenever possible, the differences between pragmatism and the liberal arts should be reconciled and a balanced undergraduate curriculum should be one of the Regents' continuing goals. The need for curricular change in schools of business and education posed a special challenge. The former are challenged to prepare graduates for competition in a global economy while at the same time protecting and preserving our natural environment. The latter is torn between pressures for further professionalization and demands for more subject matter content.

The University System was challenged to find ways in which teaching faculty could be recognized and rewarded. Alternative salary schedules should be sought in which effective classroom performance could be maintained by skilled professionals who establish student/faculty relations that are conducive to learning. To this end, the Board of Regents should review policies involving annual faculty evaluations based on the "going market rate." If current market rates are a factor in the intended salary schedule, that fact should be explicit.

The report endorsed presidential leadership and authority in matters of institutional operation and urged the Regents to "make a stronger definition" of all administrative responsibilities. In the area of planning, however, the report notes abundant evidence of plans and scarce evidence of planning results. The Board of Regents was encouraged to require that all plans for improvement be accompanied by specifications for each plan's implementation.

With respect to assessment and other forms of evaluation, the report calls attention to the use of outside experts in the surveys conducted by Works and Strayer, the stimulus of legislative committees and public commissions in the 1950s and 1960s, the federal mandate of 1202 commissions in the 1970s, and more recent deferences in the use of outside consultants in major policy decisions. Implicit in many of the report's observations is the advice that the Board of Regents not relax its guard of the Board's independence. The assessment report itself is evidence of what can be done internally, and a direct implication is the continued strengthening of the Chancellor's staff for more comprehensive responsibilities in assessment and evaluation.

REGIONAL UNIVERSITIES

In July 1990 the institutional composition of the University System was again changed by the escalation of Georgia Southern to university status. The concept of a multi-campus regional university had been proposed in 1989 as part of a systemwide effort to develop a strategic plan for public higher education in the State. The original plan included Georgia Southern, Armstrong State, Savannah State, Brunswick, and East Georgia colleges and the Skidaway Institute of Oceanography, all of which are located in the southeastern corner of the State. The rationale for the formation of a regional university included a "solution" to the "Savannah Problem" of program transfer, institutional merger, and inter-institutional cooperation. Each of the institutions would gain better control of its internal operations and thereby preserve its particular heritage. Each institution would also achieve certain academic goals dependent upon expansion of their degree programs. Establishment of a multi-campus university also would eliminate artificial barriers existing among the institutions and decrease their rivalry for students in selected academic fields. More importantly, the proposed university would expand educational opportunities for the region and give the region a more prestigious institution that could serve its particular needs. In addition, the proposed university would respond to previous efforts to establish a university in the southern half of the State.

Following approval of the concept by the Regents in January 1989 and a more intensive study of the mission and role of regional universities, a revised proposal for the establishment of regional universities was submitted in September 1989 by the Planning and Oversight Committee of the Board of Regents. The approved proposal established a Type I (Regional) category to correspond with the other two categories for funding university-level institutions and set the date for Georgia Southern's change-of-status to a regional university, with the participation of Armstrong State and Savannah State. The mission of the new university was to offer a more comprehensive array of baccalaureate degree programs, a wider range of master's and Ed.S. programs, and extensive programs at the doctoral level. The research programs of the regional university would be carefully differentiated from those of the other four universities. The term "regional" was used to specify a mission that was less-than-statewide in nature.

In July 1990 Georgia Southern officially became Georgia Southern University, with further designation as "a regional university of the University System of Georgia." In addition to being units of the University System, Armstrong State and Savannah State are officially designated "an affiliate of Georgia Southern University." Each institution maintains its autonomy as an undergraduate college but participates in the graduate and research activities of Georgia Southern. All undergraduate degrees are awarded by the respective colleges and graduate degrees are conferred by Georgia Southern University.

Administrative titles of the three presidents were changed to include status as a provost of Georgia Southern University as well as president of their respective institutions. In other words, the president of Savannah State holds the titles of president of Savannah State College *and* provost of Georgia Southern University. The president of Georgia Southern University is the chief administrative official for graduate instruction and research. Day-to-day operations, however, are the responsibility of a new position called university vice president and dean for graduate studies and research. Among the new vice president's responsibilities is the chairing of a university graduate council and a university research council. To assist in the coordination of graduate programs, an associate dean is based on the Armstrong State and Savannah State campuses. The graduate faculty of the new university consists of faculty members (with appropriate credentials) at all three institutions. Thus the new university structure and functions assure coordination in graduate studies and research, provide a more comprehensive array of educational services in the Savannah area, and involve all three institutions in providing such services to the region.

PLANNING FOR THE 1990s

In June 1990 the Board of Regents approved a comprehensive plan for the University System's continued development. The plan was the culmination of numerous studies, committee reports, and policy decisions that addressed the status and functions of public higher education in the 1980s. As its title indicates, the plan focuses on the continuing and new demands that will be placed upon the University System in the 1990s and its contents give good direction and guidance to the 34 institutions that must respond to the changing needs and expectations of the University System's many constituencies.

In responding to the needs of the State's growing population and its continuously developing economy, the plan gave good attention to the educational programs that prepare college students for productive, useful, and satisfying careers in agriculture, education, business, science, technology, and public service. As a statewide system of public higher education, the University System has unique responsibilities for the human resources that will be needed in the 1990s and in the early years of the 21st century. In responding to public demands and expectations, the plan addressed a statewide need for increasing participation in higher education. Recommendations in the plan thus dealt with ways in which: (a) students can be reached at earlier levels of education, (b) the participation of nontraditional students can be increased, (c) the retention and progression of students can be improved, and (d) the participation of minorities can be increased in all facets of public higher education.

A valuable and instructive feature of the plan is the mission statement given for the University System and the institutional roles defined for universities, senior colleges, and two-year colleges. The mission of the University System is "to promote higher learning and to advance and create knowledge." The System accomplishes its mission through its 34 institutions, their respective faculties and students, and the application of knowledge "to the state as a whole." The System's performance is to be measured by participation in its programs, services, and activities; by the impact of its programs and services; and by the efficiency with which they are provided. Among the University System's more immediate goals are a higher national ranking among its peers, status as a leading force in the State's economic development, and excellence in its graduate programs and research.

In defining the broad, general roles of comprehensive, special-purpose, and regional universities, the plan endorsed the comprehensive university's responsibilities for graduate education, professional education, baccalaureate programs, research, and public service. The doctoral programs established by regional universities should be in areas of specialization that are fully compatible with institutional mission and responsive to the demands of the communities served by the institution. Their emphasis should be on practical or applied forms of research that address regional problems and issues.

The baccalaureate programs of senior colleges should not be as comprehensive as those of the public universities, and the emphasis in faculty research should be discipline-oriented with results that are relevant to instructional effectiveness. When graduate programs are approved, they should be confined to work at the master's level in high demand areas of specialization such as business and education.

The programs of the two-year colleges are identified in terms of their relevance to other units of higher and postsecondary education. The focus should continue to be on the first two years of academic coursework for transfer credit and in preparation for advanced studies at another institution. Two-year colleges should also continue to cooperate with technical institutes in programs where general education requirements must be met. And for the foreseeable future two-year colleges were expected to be the primary provider of developmental studies for students who are inadequately prepared for higher education.

In brief, the plan's mission and role statements give valuable instruction and guidance to institutions in program planning, development, and assessment. The roles of institutions are differentiated by level of organization and by the scope or range of their multiple functions and/or purposes. Implicit in the differential roles of the 34 institutions are the many complementary ways in which they serve the larger, more significant purposes of a responsive system of public higher education.

Continuing education and applied research are two special areas in which the University System can contribute directly and substantially to the development of the State's economy and to the development of communities within the State. Other ways in which the University System will respond to the needs of state and society are: (a) extending baccalaureate programs into areas where access to college instruction has been limited, (b) meeting more effectively the needs of students for vocational, technical, and/or career-related programs of instruction and training, and (c) differentiating and coordinating the institutional roles that have been defined in the University System's structure of five universities, 14 senior colleges, and 15 two-year colleges.

A special, if not urgent, feature of the plan is its concern with the assurance and improvement of quality in programs, students, and faculty. The improvement of undergraduate education is, as stressed throughout the 1980s, the University System's greatest challenge and the coalescence of better prepared students, highly competent faculty, and well organized academic programs is the most demanding function of institutional leadership. Related to the improvement of undergraduate education is the need for better coordination in graduate and research programs. Both graduate instruction and applied research, as institutional services, are increasingly subject to the same pressures that de-centralized many aspects of undergraduate education during the 1970s and 1980s. Further challenge is seen in the University System's growing concern for evidence of institutional effectiveness. As public demands for accountability increase and as accrediting agencies place additional emphasis on the assessment of educational outcomes, assurances of improved institutional effectiveness become mandatory for all institutions of higher education.

In brief, the closing years of the 1980s should be regarded as one of the University System's most challenging stages of development. Within the brief span of two years, the presidential leadership of the System's three largest institutions changed and in rapid order major changes were again made in the System's major structure and functions. The changes observed in institutional status and leadership, in public and institutional policy, and in educational programs and services were both immediate *and* long-range challenges to the Regents and the 34 institutions they govern. The manner in which the University System responded to these various challenges is indicative of a level of maturity that was not evident in the 1950s and 1960s. The manner in which the University System itself fostered a systemwide assessment, a new university, a long range plan, and a new budgeting process recalls the recommendations made in 1963 for strengthening the central organization and administration of the Board of Regents and for emphasizing "cooperative study, long-range planning, coordination, and public advocacy of the needs of higher education." To borrow the words of President Emeritus Noah Langdale, the University System closed the decade of the 1980s, "in good condition, well led by its Chancellor, and with its interests, hopes, and promises well guarded by its Regents" (p. 56).

CHAPTER SEVEN
Status and Potential: 1990-2000

> *To understand any belief, any ideal, any custom, any*
> *institution, we must examine its gradual growth from*
> *primitive beginnings to its present form. The character of*
> *an individual and the civilization of a nation are the result*
> *of a long development. . . . Time and history are of*
> *fundamental importance.*
>
> John Herman Randall, Jr.
> *Making of the Modern Mind*, 1926

The decade of the 1990s opened with a highly optimistic outlook for the University System of Georgia. The population of Georgia had grown significantly throughout the 1980s and at least one additional representative in Congress was assured by the 1990 Census. Population projections indicated that within the first four or five years of the decade, Georgia would exceed North Carolina in population and become the nation's tenth largest state. Other demographic trends, such as the age, gender, and ethnic composition of Georgia's population, suggested that the State's social, economic, and political "growing pains" would not be as severe as those expected in other states. With such expectations, the University System of Georgia's status and potential for continued growth is indeed the result of its historical development, and its institutions, programs, and personnel do indeed reflect the fundamental importance of time, place, and origin.

In the fall of 1990 enrollments within the University System increased to 180,447 students. The relative gain in enrollment was 4.7 percent and when converted to full-time-equivalent students (n=6,026), the gain was still a substantial 4.2 percent. The relative gain for the University System, as a whole, exceeded in number of students the enrollments of all but three of the State's senior colleges. Relative increases in the junior and senior classes were appreciably higher than those observed in freshman classes. The highest relative gain, however, was at the sophomore level (14.6%). Twenty of the System's 34 institutions reported their highest enrollments of record and only four institutions within the System reported decreases in enrollment.

Over four out of ten students (43.6%) were enrolled in one of the System's five university-level institutions; slightly more than a third of the students (34.6%) were enrolled in one of fourteen senior colleges, and approximately one out of five (21.7%) were enrolled in one of the fifteen two-year colleges. When the class levels of the 180,447 students are considered, roughly one-fourth (24.5%) of the group were freshmen, less than one out of five (19.3%) were sophomores, one out of eight (12.2%) were juniors, and one out of seven (13.6%) were seniors. The remaining students were enrolled in graduate programs (13.0%) and professional degree programs (2.1%), classified as "all other" (4.0%)—or enrolled in developmental studies (11.5%). The enrollment in developmental studies represented almost one in every twelve University System students.

The University System's approved budget for the fiscal year 1990-1991 exceeded 1.7 billion dollars, an increase of almost 100 million over the previous year. Included in the budget were salaries for 9,425 faculty positions, 2,175 research positions, 5,308 public service positions, and 2,460 administrators or professional staff members. Institutional budgets for the five universities ranged from 334.8 million for the University of Georgia to 60.7 million for Georgia Southern. For the senior colleges the average institutional budget was 22.0 million dollars while the average for two-year colleges was 8.85 million. In summary, as the decade of the 1990s opened the University System operated 34 institutions of higher education, employed the full-time-equivalent of 27,529 individuals as faculty *and* staff, enrolled at least 180,447 individual students, and expended 1.7 billion dollars in providing its numerous and various programs, services, benefits, and advantages.

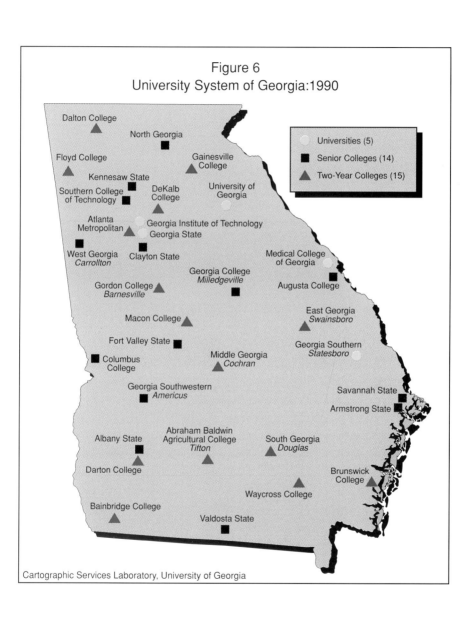

Figure 6
University System of Georgia:1990

Dalton College

North Georgia

○ Universities (5)

Floyd College

Gainesville
College

■ Senior Colleges (14)

Kennesaw State

▲ Two-Year Colleges (15)

Southern College
of Technology

DeKalb
College

University of
Georgia

Atlanta
Metropolitan

Georgia Institute of Technology
Georgia State

West Georgia   Clayton State
Carrollton

Medical College
of Georgia

Georgia College
Milledgeville

Gordon College ▲
Barnesville

Augusta College

Macon College ▲

East Georgia
Swainsboro

Fort Valley State ■

Georgia Southern
Statesboro

Columbus
College

Middle Georgia
▲ Cochran

Georgia Southwestern
■ Americus

Savannah State

Armstrong State ■

Albany State

Abraham Baldwin
Agricultural College
Tifton

South Georgia
▲ Douglas

Darton College

Brunswick
College ▲

Waycross College

Bainbridge College

Valdosta State

Cartographic Services Laboratory, University of Georgia

STATUS AND FUNCTIONS

The status of the University System's institutions, facilities, faculties, students, programs, and services (in 1990) is indicative of its potential for continued growth and development. January 1, 1992 marks sixty years of remarkable progress and service by sixteen institutions with founding dates prior to 1932. Only eleven of the sixteen, however, can claim direct descent from an ancestor on the same site. In name, location, basic structure, and general functions five institutions are comparable to their 1932 antecedents. The University of Georgia is still the state's largest and most comprehensive institution of higher education and Georgia Tech is still the state's primary technological or engineering institution. The Medical College of Georgia's title, of course, still conveys its primary mission. Two colleges—Middle Georgia College in Cochran and South Georgia College in Douglas—were residential two-year colleges in 1932 and they retained that distinction in 1990. All other institutional comparisons between 1932 and 1990 involve different paths, routes, and detours.

Mission and Roles: The specific functions of the 34 units of the University System are generally depicted by their classification as universities, senior colleges, and two-year colleges. In a national classification of institutions (CFAT, 1987), the University of Georgia and Georgia Tech are more accurately classified as major research and graduate universities. Both institutions meet standards in funded research, graduate programs, library holdings, and other assets that identify the two of them as national, as well as regional and state, resources. Georgia State is classified as a doctorate-granting university (Class I) and enjoys an enviable reputation as one of the nation's leading urban universities. The Medical College of Georgia is classified as a specialized institution (i.e., a medical college awarding most of its professional degrees in medicine). Georgia Southern was classified at the time as a comprehensive college (Class I) but would eventually be a doctorate-granting institution.

On the basis of their enrollments (over 2,500 students),
graduate work (leading to a MA degree), and bachelor degrees
(conferred in two or more professional fields) seven colleges—
Armstrong State, Augusta, Columbus, Georgia, Kennesaw,
Valdosta State, and West Georgia—were classified as comprehensive colleges (Class I). In meeting similar requirements in
baccalaureate programs but not necessarily in graduate work,
Albany State, Fort Valley State, Georgia Southwestern, North
Georgia, and Savannah State colleges were classified as comprehensive colleges (Class II). None of the public senior colleges were classified as liberal arts colleges because their course
offerings are not restricted to four-year programs in the arts,
sciences, and humanities.

All of the public two-year colleges are classified simply as
"two-year community, junior, and technical," with no distinc-
tions made between Brunswick, Bainbridge, and Dalton colleges (with their vocational-technical programs) and other two-
year institutions within the System. Variations in size are thus
more pronounced among the two-year colleges than their respective roles within the University System. DeKalb College,
with an enrollment exceeding 12,000 students, remains the largest and either Waycross or East Georgia may be identified as
the smallest.

In brief, the mission and role of each institution display its
historical development within the University System. Institutions that began as private, county, or city sponsored colleges
have altered and more or less blended their respective responsibilities with those of other units of the System. There are
noticeable variations in traditions and other institutional characteristics, but each institution serves well as an essential part
of the overall System. Together the 34 institutions offer an impressive array of educational programs and services, and the
University System itself is well described as a *comprehensive*
system of public higher education.

Resources and Facilities: The revenues and expenditures of the University System reflect the range and magnitude of its numerous functions, operations, and activities. In 1990-1991 the University System received $947.5 million (54.4%) in state appropriations; generated $409.5 million (23.5%) from student tuition and fees, gifts and grants, and other sources; earned $34.1 million through its community education and public service programs; and acquired $336.1 million (19.3%) through federal, state, local, and private grants or contracts and other sales or services. Included in the total revenues of $1,741 million were 14 million dollars as special incentive funds. Federal contracts and grants accounted for $232.9 million (13.3%) of the total budget.

Seventy-eight percent ($1,357 million) of the FY91 budget was expended on general operations. Included in such expenditures are academic support and student services (9.4%); institutional support or administrative services (9.3%); physical plant operations and maintenance (9.3%); *and* the three major responsibilities of instruction, research, and public service—for which almost half (48.9%) of the University System's total funds are expended. Not included in the general operating budget are $14 million (0.8%) for special initiative funds; $34 million (1.9%) for department services not covered in general operations; and $336 million (19.3%) for the sponsored operations of the various institutions.

The System's four major universities account for over $726 million (44.2%) of the total FY91 budget, with Georgia Southern (as the new regional university) accounting for an additional 3.4 percent. The fourteen senior colleges spend $308 million (17.6%) and the fifteen two-year colleges spend $132 million (7.6%) in carrying out their respective missions. When expenditures are displayed as general budgetary categories, personal services account for the greater proportion (70.8%) of the System's total budget; operating supplies and expenses account for 27.5 percent and the remaining 1.5 percent is expended on "other specific expenditures" such as Regents scholarships and opportunity grants.

The University System's many physical facilities are widely dispersed throughout the State. If all classrooms, libraries, laboratories, dormitories, cafeterias, gymnasiums, health services, administrative and faculty offices, and other campus buildings could be reassembled in one location, they would occupy 897.38 acres—slightly less than 14 percent of the 6,509 acres that are the campuses of 34 institutions. The total number of all such buildings is 2,481 and their value is estimated as 3.1 billion dollars. Over half (61%) of the buildings are located on or controlled by the universities; senior colleges account for 683 (27%) and two-year colleges operate with 268 (11%) of the buildings used for public higher education. Not included in the campus acreage are 45,696 acres located off campus and used primarily by the University of Georgia (43,334) and Fort Valley State (1,338), the State's two landgrant institutions.

When uses of physical facilities are considered, almost 39 percent of the floor space is used for academic and/or instructional purposes, 6.7 percent is used for administrative reasons, 18 percent is used for faculty and student support services of various kinds, and the remaining 37 percent is used for innumerable "other" purposes (such as service buildings, rental property, parking decks). When the academic/instructional uses of physical facilities are considered, the University System uses 2,180 classrooms and 5,031 laboratories, plus 136 other rooms for continuing education. Laboratories are classified as teaching labs (24%), nonteaching labs (33%), and research labs (43%). The recency of the University System's rapid growth is shown by the fact that 1,527 (61%) of its 2,481 buildings have been constructed since 1965. Twenty-six buildings, however, are over one hundred years old and 217 buildings (8%) were constructed between 1890 and 1940.

In its quest for academic excellence, one of the University System's best investments can be seen in its campus libraries.

Over 15 million dollars were spent in FY90 on acquisitions, and total holdings in books, documents, and microfilm exceeded 28.4 million. The value of library holdings within units of the University System exceeded 202 million dollars. Almost six out of every ten books (59.2%) are in the university libraries of the System. The University of Georgia library contained almost three million volumes and was ranked 23rd among the nation's libraries in 1989. The Georgia Tech library contained over 1.6 million volumes and was ranked 103 at the same time. Regionally the University of Georgia library is ranked fifth and is surpassed in holdings only by the universities of Texas, North Carolina, Virginia, and Duke University. Georgia Tech ranks 22nd among southern universities. Together the university libraries of the University System hold over 6.2 million volumes while the senior colleges account for 3.2 million (31.0%) and the two-year colleges account for over one million volumes (9.7%). In brief, the library holdings of institutions within the University System are among its most impressive accomplishments.

Faculties: The faculties of its 34 institutions are a major asset in all considerations of the University System's status and potential. At least 8,146 faculty members (in 1990) engaged in the instructional, research, and service programs of their institutions, and each contributed directly or indirectly to the progress of public higher education in Georgia. The talents, expertise, and commitments of the University System's faculties signify an area of responsibility in which the quest for self-reliance is most evident. With few exceptions, the public universities of Georgia now have the resources and capabilities to educate, train, and develop the faculty members needed at all levels of higher education.

   Considered as a group, the faculties of the University System are scholars, scientists, and professional specialists with commendable credentials in the physical and biological sciences, the behavioral and social sciences, the humanities and fine arts, and the diverse professional and applied fields that are encompassed by undergraduate, graduate, and professional education. Sixty-four percent of the faculty members have earned a doctoral degree and an additional 6 percent hold the highest professional degree in their respective fields of specialization. Thirty-one percent of the faculty members are women, many of whom teach in two-year colleges where they represent 47.5 percent of the teaching faculties. Eight percent of the University System's faculty members are black minority members, but four out of ten minority faculty members hold appointments at the public historically black institutions.

An appreciation of faculty competence and performance may be gleaned from statistical data that are gathered routinely. Over half (57%) of the full-time faculty members have tenure and at least 56 percent of them hold senior rank as full or associate professors. Over 4,600 faculty members (56.5%) hold rank at one of the five universities where they have met additional standards imposed by peer review in promotion and tenure decisions. At least 36 percent of the faculty members hold rank at a senior college and approximately 13 percent of them hold rank within a two-year college. At the senior college level 28 percent of the faculty are full professors while in the two-year colleges only 14 percent hold the rank of full professor.

Over 1,454 university faculty members (36%) are full professors while their colleagues serve as associate professors (31%), assistant professors (28%), and instructors (5%). The salaries earned by university faculty are determined, for the most part, by academic discipline or professional specialty, faculty rank, length of service, the prestige of institutions granting their highest degree, and the mission of the institution at which they currently serve. Thus, in 1991 the average full-time faculty salaries were $44,859 at the University of Georgia, $48,403 at Georgia Tech and Georgia State, and $36,063 at Georgia Southern. Salaries at the University of Georgia and Georgia Southern were below the regional average for comparable universities while salaries at Georgia Tech and Georgia State were above the regional average for similar institutions.

For senior colleges offering work at the master's level, the average full-time faculty salary of $36,888 was above the regional average but below the national average. For senior colleges offering work at the baccalaureate level only (Clayton State), the average full-time faculty salary of $35,529 was above the regional average but not the national average. Faculty salaries at the fifteen two-year colleges averaged $32,304 and were slightly above the regional average for comparable colleges. Only at Georgia Tech and Georgia State were faculty salaries above the national average for similar or comparable institutions of higher education (Marks, 1991).

In brief, there have been many remarkable changes in the faculties of Georgia's public universities and colleges since the severe faculty shortage of the 1960s. The post-WWII faculties who were hastily recruited to teach returning veterans were often replaced by many of their own students, and throughout the 1980s the veterans were replaced by students they had taught in the 1960s. Faculty development policies of "grow your own" have been successful and neither the University System nor the private colleges of Georgia are overly dependent upon other states or regions for faculty and professional staffs.

Students: The number and diversity of students in the 1990s make a striking contrast with the 8,035 students enrolled in 1933. In the fall of 1990 the students enrolled in units of the University System were still predominantly white (80.2%) but an increasing number of them (15.7%) were black and an appreciable number of others (4.1%) were members of other racial or ethnic groups. Except for the universities where over half (51.1%) are men, the majority of students in the University System are women (54.9%) and many of them enroll on a part-time basis (36.3%). As undergraduates, students in 1990 were older—with an average age of 23.2 years—and in the public two-year colleges the typical student was almost 25 years old.

A total of 78,698 students (43.6%) were enrolled in the five public universities. The enrollment of the University of Georgia

(28,395) was as large as the University System's enrollment in 1958. The separate enrollments of four universities, one senior college (Kennesaw State), and one two-year college (DeKalb) exceeded the University System's enrollment in its first four years of operation. Together the fifteen two-year colleges enrolled more students than the entire University System did until 1964 when the baby-boomers first arrived.

The great majority of students (81.1%) were still enrolled in undergraduate programs, but 11.5 percent of the University System's students were taking courses in developmental studies and would not receive degree-credit for their efforts. The dramatic increase in graduate enrollments was displayed by 23,536 students who represented 13.0 percent of the System's total enrollment. When compared to the State's increased population since 1930, student enrollments are less dramatic but nonetheless indicative of the University System's remarkable growth. In 1933 the ratio of students (8,035) to population (2.9 million) was .0025 and suggests that for every ten thousand Georgians 25 students were enrolled in a unit of the University System. In 1990 the ratio of students to population (6.4 million) was .0272 and suggested an attendance of 272 students for every ten thousand Georgians. Thus, the highly significant increases in student enrollments since 1932 are the best single indication of the University System's effectiveness in meeting the educational needs of Georgia citizens and residents.

The abilities and achievement of entering freshmen are indicative of the changing demands and challenges to which institutions of higher learning must respond. In 1989 the average SAT-Verbal score recorded for entering University System freshmen was 417 and the average SAT-Mathematics score was 455. When interpreted as an index of verbal and mathematical abilities related to effective learning in college courses, SAT scores convey useful and valuable information about the readiness of entering students for the intellectual and academic challenges of college instruction. The average SAT scores of students entering Georgia Tech, Georgia State, and the University of Georgia, thus interpreted, suggest appreciable preparation for college and predictable success in meeting course requirements and instructor expectations. The average scores recorded for students in senior and two-year colleges suggest a lesser degree of verbal and mathematical ability but at least half of the students entering such institutions should not have undue difficulty in meeting academic standards.

A similar interpretation of educational achievement can be made from the high school grades reported for entering University System freshmen. In 1989 the mean high school average for entering freshmen was 2.6 (on a 4.0 scale), a level of academic performance that would be regarded as typical or average in most high schools. Averages are misleading, however, and a better interpretation of student abilities and achievement can be made from the distribution of SAT scores and high school grades. In the fall of 1989 less than 12 percent of the entering freshmen came with "A" or "B+" averages in high school; over 16 percent entered with high school grades averaging "D" or lower. The remaining 72 percent, of course, had earned high school averages in the middle range of the grade distribution.

The distribution of SAT scores discloses three distinct levels of verbal and mathematical ability. In 1989 less than 5 percent (4.1%) of the University System's entering freshmen scored above 600 on the SAT-Verbal scale. Almost exactly half (50.5%) scored in the mid-range between 400 and 600, and 45.2 percent (12,188 students) scored below 400. On the SAT-Mathematics scale 11.7 percent scored above 600 while 55.4 percent scored between 400 and 600 and 33.0 percent scored below 400 points. Student scores on the two scales suggest better preparation in mathematics than in verbal reasoning, vocabulary, and reading comprehension. Such an interpretation is attenuated, however, by recognition that half of the students (48%) with high SAT-Mathematics are at Georgia Tech where admission policies emphasize mathematical ability. This alone could account for the differences in scores above 600 and the average differences between SAT-Verbal and SAT-Mathematics scores.

If SAT-Verbal scores are accepted as the most easily obtained indication of how well entering students will perform in
English, history, political science, sociology, and other first-
year courses requiring extensive reading, the distribution of
SAT-Verbal scores implies that well prepared freshmen are far
out-numbered by poorly prepared freshmen. Less than 5 percent of the 1989 entering students scored 600 or higher on the
verbal section of the SAT. Given the admission of 12,188 students who scored below 400 on the SAT-Verbal scale, the enrollment in developmental studies of 19,729 students (11.4% of
the total System enrollment) followed as a logical consequence
of inadequate high school preparation.

In summary, the abilities and achievement of entering students imply that the excellence of the University System, *as* a
statewide system of public higher education, is limited by the
quality of education in the public schools. Commendable progress
has been made in establishing a college preparatory curriculum, but three out of every ten freshmen have not completed a
preparatory program of study. In the first three years of additional curricular requirements for admission, the effectiveness
of the college preparatory curriculum was not demonstrated by
rates of completion or by prevention of placement in developmental studies. The program was effective, nonetheless, in identifying more quickly the academic deficiencies of students and
in facilitating their exit from developmental studies (Hudson
and Pounds, 1991).

The assessment of student abilities and achievement at
higher levels is implied by the Regents Test (for sophomores)
and exit examinations (for seniors). The passing rates for sophomores more or less confirm the reading and writing difficulties
of beginning students, but the systemwide passing rate of 74.9
percent does not convey useful information about students and
their basic academic competencies. Institutional passing rates
ranging from 28.5 percent to 88.2 percent tell more about problems in dealing with unprepared students than about institutional effectiveness in teaching basic skills of literacy. Thus,

variations in student abilities and institutional policies, programs, and services imply that the assessment of educational outcomes in the form of academic competencies, general achievement, or advanced learning skills remains a major challenge for both the University System and its institutions.

Academic Programs: The range and diversity of curricula within the University System are further testament to its effectiveness in responding to changing demands and expectations. Vestiges of a traditional curriculum are apparent in core curriculum requirements for the humanities, natural sciences, and mathematics but the substance and content of undergraduate courses have changed significantly since the 1950s. Most baccalaureate programs consist of general education courses in the freshmen and sophomore years, with advanced or specialized coursework in the junior and senior years, but many bachelor's degrees take five years for completion.

The great diversity of program and course offerings are depicted in college catalogs, by the majors declared by students, and by the degrees conferred by institutions. The bachelor of arts degree and the bachelor of science degree are still the most frequently awarded degrees, but the areas of specialization are innumerable. For the University System, twelve broadly grouped areas of specialization encompass the declared majors of 72 percent of the students. The fields in which students declare majors are: agriculture, business, computer science, education, engineering (and engineering technology), foreign languages, humanities and fine arts, mathematics, nursing, allied health specialties, life sciences, physical sciences, and social sciences. Computer science, engineering technology, and allied health specialties are the most conspicuous additions to the curriculum since the 1950s. Business (22.6%), education (8.2%), and health specialties (9.3%) are the most frequently identified areas. Traditional major fields in foreign languages (0.9%), mathematics (0.9%), physical sciences (1.4%) are not identified as frequently as those in the humanities and fine arts (4.5%) and the life sciences (3.4%). Agriculture, engineering, mathematics, and foreign languages are fields identified by less than one percent each of the University System students, but one percent of over 112,000 undergraduates is a significant number of students.

The number of degrees conferred in areas of specialization indicates, to an appreciable degree, both student demand and institutional productivity. In 1988-1989 the four universities conferred 12,750 degrees, the senior colleges conferred 9,863 degrees, and the two-year colleges awarded 3,204 associate degrees. The total for the University System was 25,817 degrees. The fields of specialization in which degrees were conferred are comparable to the areas in which students declare majors. Together the twelve areas (in which majors are declared) encompass 85 percent of the bachelor's degrees conferred. Almost one out of three bachelor's degrees (31.5%) were conferred in business. Education (12.7%), engineering/engineering technology (10.8%), and the social sciences (10.9%) account for another third of the conferred degrees. And computer science (3.4%), foreign languages (0.5%), humanities and fine arts (3.2%), mathematics (1.1%); nursing and health specialties (0.5%), life sciences (2.3%), and physical sciences (1.4%) account for an additional one out of eight degrees. The remaining degrees (15.1%) were awarded in other areas of specialization such as architecture, communications, home economics, social services, and general studies.

Bachelor's and master's degrees are conferred by both universities and senior colleges. The public universities confer approximately 54 percent of the baccalaureates granted within the System and 66 percent of the master's degrees. Senior colleges, for which the master's degree is their highest degree, confer 46 percent of the System's baccalaureates and 34 percent of the System's master's degrees.

Business, education, engineering, and the social sciences are areas of specialization in which significant numbers of bachelor's, master's, and doctoral degrees are conferred. Indeed, business and education continue to be the fields in which University System students are most likely to earn degrees. In

1988-1989, business majors received 31.5 percent of the bachelor's degrees, 21.2 percent of the master's degrees, and 7.8 percent of the doctoral degrees. Education majors received 12.7 percent of the bachelor's degrees, 37.8 percent of the master's, and 32.0 percent of the doctoral degrees. Engineering and engineering technology accounted for 10.8 percent of the bachelor's degrees, 9.4 percent of the master's, and 13.7 percent of the doctoral degrees. And the social sciences (with psychology) accounted for 11.1 percent of the bachelor's, 4.9 percent of the master's, and 10.3 percent of the doctoral degrees. Together these four areas of specialization accounted for 66.1 percent of all baccalaureates, 73.3 percent of all master's degrees, and 63.8 percent of all doctorates.

In brief, the 34 institutions of the University System provide a comprehensive and commendable array of academic degrees, programs, and courses to serve the educational needs and interests of Georgians. Business, education, engineering, and the social sciences are the preferred areas of advanced or specialized education, however, and the frequency of declared majors and conferred degrees in such fields is indicative of the practical learning needs and interests that characterize American higher education. The arts, sciences, and humanities are represented well in the degree programs of the University System, but they are chosen (as major fields of study) by a minority of the System's upper-division and graduate students.

In essence, the curricular offerings of the public universities, senior colleges, and two-year colleges are their major assets and their primary reason-for-being. Admission policies, program standards, and course requirements are conducive to the fair-and-equitable use of the University System's resources by Georgia citizens and residents. During the years 1966-1976 when undergraduate education was subjected to radical change, the University System was spared many ineffective curricular revisions that were masked as innovative reforms. On many occasions the University System's leadership and policies acted as a much needed flywheel. Within the University System, as elsewhere, there are profound changes yet to be fully assimilated and there are many ways in which undergraduate teaching *and* learning can be improved. Arbitrary program standards, course requirements, and instructor expectations persist, but the development of academic programs and courses is responsive to the changing needs and demands of the University System's many constituencies. By avoiding mistakes that other institutions of higher education have made, the University System maintains a more favorable position to plan and develop effectively the academic programs and services that will be needed to meet public expectations in the 1990s.

Public Service and Research: The University System's commitment to public service is clearly seen in its numerous continuing education, inservice training, short-term instruction, and professional development programs for citizens and residents who are not formally enrolled as students in one of the public universities, senior colleges, or two-year colleges. Commitment and effectiveness are further demonstrated in the various functions and activities of the Georgia Center for Continuing Education (UGA), the Cooperative Extension Service (UGA), the Rural Development Center (Tifton), the Economic Development Laboratory (GT), and the Urban Life Center (GSU). The nature and extent of its many services to state, county, or municipal government and to local communities are evident in the work of Institute of Government (UGA), the Institute of Community and Area Development (UGA), the Economic Forecasting Center (GSU), and various other institutes or centers with missions related to the State's social, economic, political, and technological development.

In addition to many institutes and centers with explicit responsibilities for working with the University System's public constituencies, numerous programs, projects, and activities are sponsored and conducted by USGA institutions and their various divisions. In FY89 almost 12,000 programs, involving over 250,000 participants, were planned, organized, and conducted

by units of the System's 34 institutions. The productivity of
such public service programs is evident from the generation of
almost 7,000 continuing education units (CEU's). Almost a third
(30.8%) of these programs were conducted by the four universities; over four out of ten (43.2%) were conducted by the senior
colleges and the remaining 25.9 percent was conducted by the
two-year colleges. The extent and variety of such programs reflect a commendable responsiveness to public perceptions of
the State's colleges and universities as an available source of
personal, social, professional, and technical assistance.

The research programs, projects, and activities of contem-
porary universities defy brief description and resist logical categories by which their various objectives and outcomes can be
consistently displayed. In 1990-1991 the University System budgeted over $101 million for the full-time equivalent of 2,175
positions. In its allocation of research positions to institutions,
the University System staffs research institutes and centers that
generate almost $300 million annually in research funds. By
delegating its responsibilities for research to the universities,
the University System supports their research mission and fa-
cilitates the discovery, dissemination, and use of knowledge in
service to state and nation.

The division of research responsibilities is shown by the
expenditure of over $271.7 million in FY89. The University of
Georgia expended over $104 million (38.2%) in research funds,
while Georgia Tech spent at least $136.8 million (50.3%). Georgia
State spent $16.1 million (5.9%) and the Medical College spent
$14.7 million (5.4%). Distinctive research facilities and programs
for the University of Georgia are the Complex Carbohydrate Research Center, the Advanced Computational Methods Center,
the Computational Quantum Chemistry Center, the Savannah
River Ecology Laboratory, the Marine Institute on Sapelo Is-
land, the Skidaway Institute of Oceanography, and the Agricultural Experimental Stations—with three main stations at Griffin, Tifton, and Athens, and five branch stations at Blairsville,
Calhoun, Eatonton, Midville, and Plains.

Distinctive facilities and programs for Georgia Tech are the
Georgia Tech Research Institute, which consists of seven major
research laboratories, the Microelectronics Research Center, the
Health Systems Research Center, and the Technology Policy
and Assessment Center. Georgia State conducts most of its research within its colleges of Arts and Sciences, Business, Health
Sciences, Public and Urban Affairs, and Education but may
boast of its Language Research Center and its program on comparative primate cognition, its Economic Policy Center, and its
Center for High Angular Resolution Astronomy. The Medical
College takes pride in the Alzheimers Basic and Clinical Research Center, the Comprehensive Sickle Cell Center, the Georgia Institute of Human Nutrition, and the Georgia Institute for
Prevention of Human Disease and Accidents.

National rankings of Georgia Tech and the University of
Georgia reflect their increasing national recognition as major
research universities. In terms of research and development
funds received from the federal government, Georgia Tech (in
1988) was ranked 46th in the nation while the University of Georgia was ranked 64th. On actual expenditures for research (irre-
spective of source), both institutions rank within the nation's
top fifty research universities. The productivity and effectiveness of research are implied but not documented by national
reputations and the amount of funds expended. The potential
contributions of research often depend on cultural readiness,
public enlightenment, or technological innovations in dissemination. The range and diversity of the University System's research mission is nonetheless impressive and the remarkable
progress made since the mid-1960s underscores an auspicious
investment in Georgia's institutions of public higher education.

When considered in their entirety, the public service and
research programs of the University System substantiate and enhance the multiple purposes of public higher education. The development and effective use of human knowledge, competence,
and understanding is essential to the realization of individual

and institutional purposes—and to the technological and cultural advancement of state and society.

Intangible Resources: In addition to its commendable physical facilities, faculties, students, programs, and services, the University System has many resources that are intangible but nonetheless essential to its continued development. Primary among such resources are the status and prestige of the Regents as a single, unified governing board for Georgia's institutions of higher learning. The formulation and coalescence of public and institutional policy for 34 institutions, varying in size from the University of Georgia to Waycross College, is an awesome challenge but it is a challenge for which the Board of Regents has good experience and a record of accomplishment. The public endorsement and reinforcement of the Board's authority and responsibility, following political interference in the 1940s, is still an illustrative lesson in state politics. In similar manner, the many events accompanying or following the desegregation crises of the 1960s testify that Georgia's institutions of public higher education do not serve at the pleasure of governors and state legislators.

Leadership is an intangible resource that is always vital. Within the Board of Regents, the Chancellorship, and the institutions themselves, strong leadership has often emerged to meet the crisis at hand. In turn, governing policies and decisions give guidance and direction to many institutional decisions and actions that are responsive and adaptive. Institutions of higher education thrive best when granted reasonable autonomy and freedom in the administration of internal processes, operations, and activities that do not require major policy decisions. In other words, leadership has occasionally been late but leadership has usually arrived in time to avoid many of the tragic blunders that mar higher education in other states and other systems.

The dedication and commitments of innumerable individuals within the University System's constituencies are another valuable but intangible resource. Among the faculties, staffs, alumni, and benefactors of the various institutions are many individuals who serve public higher education well. Alumni, in particular, promote the best interests of their respective institutions and make many valuable contributions. Many faculty members teach, research, and serve well without dissent or fanfare. And staff members of all institutions serve in many effective ways as intermediaries for students and other clients.

At their worst, community pride and boosterism reflect institutional aspirations that do not always serve the University System well. At their best, however, community pride and support give colleges and universities another perspective on institutional mission and serve, on many occasions, as a buffer against forms of adversity that do not reach the rooms of governing boards. The vitality and effectiveness of institutions, programs, and services are often influenced in unpublicized but meaningful ways. Such influences are only partially evident in community service programs or in the enthusiasm that comes with national championships in intercollegiate athletics. As an intangible resource, community investments in local institutions serve in the long run to foster a climate for educational progress and advancement.

GROWTH AND ADVERSITY

The potential of the University System for continued development is inherent in its progress and improvement for well over a half century. The growth patterns of the past are readily depicted in five distinct periods of growth and development that signify substantive and enduring change. In each period of growth (or stage of development) the University System was one assemblage of institutions, personnel, programs, and services in the beginning and another in the end. In each stage of development the University System encountered adversities that delayed the advantages and benefits of higher education for many Georgia residents and citizens. And in each stage, with minor exceptions, progress was marked by increased enrollments, better programs, extended services, and more competent personnel. Setbacks have indeed been a part of each stage of development but growth, progress, and improvement have been explicit throughout the University System's history.

In retrospect, 1932-1950 were years of trial-and-error in which there were few guiding precedents for developing a statewide system of higher education with severely limited resources. Growth of the new University System was also hampered by deep-seated convictions that Georgia was a poor state and would remain a poor state. Nonetheless there was an increasing awareness of the value of higher education in the State's social, economic, and political advancement. Despite poverty, political interference, loss of accreditation, and World War II the University System benefitted substantially from federal assistance in buildings and programs—and from the Works and Strayer reports that defined educational liabilities and deficits.

The years 1950-1964 began with reasons for despair and closed with an optimistic outlook that the University System had not known before *or* since. Anti-intellectualism, a reactionary political climate, and uncertain economic growth in the early 1950s did not portend the "growth psychology" that characterized the early 1960s. The prospects for federal assistance, the removal of desegregation shackles, the baby-boomers, and the space age were contributory factors nationally and regionally. Equally significant was a new and different attitude toward higher education and its role in the development of human capital.

A brief growth period from 1964 to 1972 encompasses the University System's most exciting years *and* its most frightening years. The establishment of new colleges, the development of new programs, and the recruitment of new faculties proceeded at a pace that no one had anticipated. The "massive" federal funding of the 1960s and a "break-through" in state funding in 1968 were part of a floodtide that reached rocky shores almost immediately. In that brief period, however, the University System enrolled 8,028 additional students each year and grew at an annual rate of 18 percent.

The financial crisis of the early 1970s found the University System with many added responsibilities and its only serious loss of public confidence. Public policy dictated the centralization of numerous institutional policy decisions as the federal government placed a heavy emphasis on institutional planning, management, and evaluation. National enrollment projections depicted a future in which traditional college-age students (18-22 years) would be a minority, and virtually all national conferences included at least one session on nontraditional students and/or adult learners. Thus the years of 1972-1984 were a growth period in which the financial exigencies of higher education dictated an inordinate concern with accountability, managerial efficiency, cost-effectiveness, and other concepts borrowed from the nation's business corporations. Unfortunately for institutions of public higher education, national objectives and priorities encouraged hastily planned programs of study for a new generation of students. One noted outcome of the effort was an erosion of academic standards on many college campuses.

The University System's fifth growth period (1984-1990) witnessed a rapid turnover in institutional leadership, a loosening of centralized control, and a re-emergence of institutional aspirations. Changes in leadership brought changes in administrative styles *and* the commitments of institutional leaders to previous plans and policies. Enrollments expanded in unprecedented ways, and institutional missions changed with or without deliberate planning and policy decisions. A noticeable characteristic of the late 1980s was the unevenness with which the institutions of the University System grew and developed. Like sectors of the national economy, institutions with fortunate growth patterns fared well while institutions with disadvantages were disadvantaged further.

Embedded in the University System's growth patterns were many irregular, uneven, and unexpected developments. No observer, critical or uncritical, would contend that the University System of Georgia is the work of a master planner or the result of grand design. A crucial factor, therefore, is the absence of any period in which there were sustained efforts to retrench or to control growth and expansion across institutions and across programs. There have been years in which financial support was reduced temporarily and a slower growth rate was evident, but reductions in financial support have always been a function of state revenues and not deliberate policy decisions.

Much of the University System's growth is related, of course, to growth in the State of Georgia's population and economy. In 1930, as mentioned previously, the population of Georgia was less than three million people and until 1960 when the population had grown to almost four million, the State's growth in population was seldom a factor in educational thought and discussion. Having taken three decades to reach 3.9 million, Georgia's population gained an additional 2.5 million in the next thirty years. The growth of the State's economy is seen in similar statistics. As *per capita* income has increased and approached the national average, so have state appropriations for higher education. In 1989 the State's *per capita* income of $16,188 was 8 percent below the national average ($17,567). State appropriations *per capita* were 10 percent below the national average.

Much to the misfortune of public higher education, the University System's budget was significantly reduced both in FY90 and FY91 as the result of a lingering recession in the State's economy. Once again the University System had entered a "stage of development" with expectations that were suddenly altered. And once again public perceptions of the University System's needs were at variance with public demands for its programs and services. The University System's resources and capabilities were indeed essential to the State's economic, technological, and cultural advancement but improvement of institutions, facilities, programs, and services was not a priority in the midst of declining state revenues.

PERENNIAL ISSUES

The University System's potential contributions to state and society are numerous, and its commitments to the intellectual, technological, and cultural advancement of individuals and institutions are encouraging. In both its contributions and commitments, the University System's experience in coping with its "perennial issues" is a factor to be considered. In higher education, as elsewhere, success in meeting one challenge leads quickly to another challenge.

Looking back, it is obvious that the University System has met the challenge of distributing geographically its institutions, programs, and services. Further challenge is apparent, however, in making higher education demographically accessible as well as geographically available. In other words, more programs and services should be within the reach of people who live in heavily concentrated areas, as well as those who live in isolated rural areas of the State. The geographical proximity of other institutions should not influence unduly the establishment of extension centers, resident graduate centers, and new institutions when the adult learner population warrants additional or other kinds of educational opportunities.

University System policies and programs have dealt with the perennial issue of unprepared students in at least five notable efforts. One of the reasons for adopting the SAT was to identify students needing academic assistance. Later a college preparatory curriculum was adopted to strengthen secondary preparation in English, mathematics, and science. Developmental studies programs were mandated as a concerted effort to remedy academic deficiencies and a college placement exam was developed to facilitate placement in courses appropriate for the different levels of student achievement. And a systemwide test of basic skills has been required to ensure standards of academic competence in transferring to upper division coursework. The University System's efforts in all five programs has been instructive and beneficial, but the challenge of teaching basic skills to educationally disadvantaged students remains the dominant "perennial issue" in public higher education.

The provision of general education to students interested in advanced, specialized, or technical programs is a challenge as old as that of assisting unprepared students. Virtually all critics of higher education deplore excessive specialization and advocate a broader diffusion of general knowledge and information to college graduates. Graduate schools, employers, and society at large, however, tend strongly to recognize those who specialize in technical or advanced fields of knowledge. The University System's core curriculum assures that students will take courses in English, mathematics, history, and science but the benefits of a general or liberal education still escape far too many college graduates. The dominance of business, education, engineering, and social science in declaring majors and earning degrees is indicative of a continuing challenge and/or issue in undergraduate education.

The challenge of curricular revision is obscured by the gradual, incremental changes that take place continuously in course content and substance. Undergraduate curricula, in particular, are changed as course requirements and faculty expectations are altered through daily lectures and class discussions. As a result, the guidance and direction of curricular change is a perennial issue at all levels of academic governance. And indeed, the most encumbersome process in higher education may be the review and approval of proposals for new courses and degree programs. Quite often the name of a division, school, or college will not be changed until long after its curriculum has undergone gradual but nonetheless profound changes. Not until 1991 did the University of Georgia's College of Agriculture become the College of Agricultural and Environmental Sciences; the College of Home Economics became the College of Family and Consumer Sciences only one year earlier.

Business, education, engineering, technology, and health care are areas of specialization in which curricular planning and development are particularly relevant. Pressures for curricular change are intense because each field of specialization is influenced significantly by changing public demands and technological innovations. The arts, sciences, and humanities are under similar pressure to "internationalize" undergraduate curricula by giving better coverage to other societies and cultures. Other conditions fostering planned-and-directed change in college and university curricula are international competition in a global economy, the economic unification of western Europe, and the acceleration of technological and sociocultural change in international relations. All things considered, the guidance and direction of curricular change in the 1990s may be the University System's greatest challenge in the remaining years of the 20th century.

In summary, the potential of the University System for continued development—despite adversities—is enormous. As a statewide system of institutions, programs, services, and professional personnel, the University System does not have the overwhelming challenges, grudging support, or overshadowing competition (of private institutions) as higher education in other states so often have. Neither does the University System run the risk of self-satisfaction from having always been in the nation's top ranked institutions of higher education. Much to the contrary, there is much in the University System's growth and development that suggests a state of becoming, a state in which much is promising and much is still possible.

As the historical development of the University System clearly demonstrates, the responsiveness of institutions of higher education to public needs, demands, and expectations is essential to their mission and role in state and society. As a statewide system of public higher education, the University System has served well its many constituencies and its state, region, and nation. The institutions, personnel, programs, services, and activities of the University System have contributed significantly and substantially to the State's social, economic, and political development. Public perceptions and expectations now imply that the University System and its 34 institutions must play a larger, more significant role in the State and region's continued economic, technological, and cultural advancement.

Annotated Bibliography

CHAPTER ONE
REORGANIZATION AND COORDINATION: 1932-1943

Allen, Ivan (Chairman). Governor's Commission To Simplify and Coordinate the Operations of Governmental Departments. *Plan of Simplification and Coordination of the Departments, Boards, Commissions, and Institutions of the State Government of Georgia.* Atlanta: State of Georgia Executive Department, 1929.

The report that laid the legal-political groundwork for the reorganization of state government during the Richard B. Russell, Jr. administration. The chairman was a prominent Atlanta businessman.

Annual Reports from Regents of the University System of Georgia: 1932-1989.

Presented annually by the chairman of the Board of Regents to the Governor. Early issues contain invaluable information about the decisions and actions of the Board in establishing the University System. Format and coverage were altered somewhat with the 1964-1965 report and editorial style was changed significantly in the late 1980s. Contain valuable data on annual budgets, enrollments, and faculty.

Brittain, M.L. *The Story of Georgia Tech.* Chapel Hill: University of North Carolina Press, 1948.

A history of Georgia Tech from the perspective of a president emeritus. Brittain was president from 1922 to 1944 and was quite familiar with the events of re-organization in 1932 and the events of 1941-1942. Includes the complete act establishing the Board of Regents. Brittain was 78 years old when he retired in 1944.

Brooks, Robert Preston. *The University of Georgia Under Sixteen Administrations: 1785-1955.* Athens: University of Georgia Press, 1956.

An administrative history of UGA by an active participant who served as dean of business, dean of faculties, alumni secretary, and director of two institutes. Gives a good account of the founding of the University System and a personal account of the "Cocking Affair." Also gives enrollment and financial data.

Candler, C. Murphey (Chairman). *Report of State Survey Committee.* Atlanta: State of Georgia Executive Department, 1925.

A Citizens Committee appointed by Governor Clifford Walker to survey "the condition and needs of our Educational System and institutions." The committee looked at the "common schools," A&M schools and junior colleges, and "the higher education institutions."

Coffman, L.D., Elliott, Edward C., Judd, Charles H., Zook, George F., and Works, George A. (Chairman). *Report to the Board of Regents of the University System of Georgia.* Atlanta: USGA, 1933.

The first of the statewide survey reports prepared by an outside group of experts is known as "the First Works Report." Contains valuable information about the early years of the Board of Regents and its responsibilities for units of the University System.

Cottingham, James A. *Patterns of Governance: A Study of the Establishment of the University System of Georgia, 1931-1943.* Doctoral Dissertation, University of Georgia, 1990.

A recent study of the University System's early years and the leadership of the Regents in decisions to close, merge, or re-organize the units inherited from their various boards of trustees. Also reviews the political events of 1941-1942.

Dorsey, Hugh M. (Governor and Chairman). *Report of Budget and Investigating Commission.* Atlanta: State of Georgia Executive Department, 1919.

Contains the earliest reference we have to a "State Board of Regents" for higher education and states the case for economies that would be effected by having only one board.

Dyer, Thomas G. *The University of Georgia: A Bicentennial History (1785-1985).* Athens: The University of Georgia Press, 1985.

An excellent interpretation of turning points in the University's history: the civil war and reconstruction, the rise of land-grant colleges, the creation of the Board of Regents, the merger of the agricultural and education colleges with the University, the "Cocking Affair," the enrollment of thousands of World War II veterans, and the University's desegregation in 1961.

Works, George A. (Director). *Report to the Board of Regents of the University System of Georgia 1943.* Atlanta: USGA, 1943.

The second survey report is known as "the Second Works Report." Funds for this study were acquired in 1940 but completion of the report was delayed by the University System's "time of troubles" in 1941-1942.

CHAPTER TWO
STATUS AND AUTHORITY: 1941-1945

Best, Jenny Warlick. *Characteristics and Activities of Georgia College and University Regents and Trustees.* Doctoral Dissertation, University of Georgia, 1988.

Provides interesting information on the individuals who serve as Regents in the University System of Georgia or as trustees for private colleges and universities within the State. Only ten of the fifteen Regents completed the survey instrument but at least three of the responding ten Regents also served on Boards of Trustees.

Board of Regents of the University System of Georgia. *The Policy Manual* (2nd ed.). Atlanta: USGA, 1982.

Supplemented monthly after each Regents meeting in which revisions in policy may have been made. Contains much useful information about the organization, administration, and governance of the University System and its various units.

Committee of the Southern Association of Colleges and Secondary Schools. *Report on University System of Georgia.* (December 3, 1941).

Summarizes the events leading up to the public hearing held in Atlanta and states succinctly the findings, conclusions, and recommendations of the committee. The committee report is reprinted in its entirety in the 1941 *Annual Report;* M.L. Brittain's, *Story of Georgia Tech;* R.P. Brooks', *University of Georgia;* and elsewhere.

Cook, James F., Jr. *Politics and Education in the Talmadge Era: The Controversy over the University System of Georgia, 1941-1942*. Doctoral Dissertation, University of Georgia, 1972.

An objective study of political interference in the affairs of the University System and the best source of information about some of the events of 1941-1942. Valuable for the interviews conducted (in later years) with some of the active participants.

Gosnell, Cullen B. *Government and Politics of Georgia*. New York: Thomas Nelson and Sons, 1936.

A general introduction to the politics, state government, and economic issues of the 1930s. The author was an advocate of better state government and an astute observer of state politics.

Orr, Dorothy. *A History of Education in Georgia*. Chapel Hill: University of North Carolina Press, 1950.

Written by the granddaughter of Georgia's first (post-reconstruction) state school superintendent with valuable information about the founding of Georgia's public school system, the state's A&M schools, and institutions of higher education. Contains biographical sketches of early educators.

Saye, Albert Berry. *A Constitutional History of Georgia*. Athens: University of Georgia Press, 1948.

A thorough discussion of Georgia's several constitutions, their contents and provisions, and the continuing need for amendments and revisions.

CHAPTER THREE
EXPANSION AND IMPROVEMENT: 1946-1960

Committee on Manpower and Education, *Special Reports*. Atlanta: Governor's Conference on Education, 1959.

Four special reports dealing with: (1) testing, counseling, and guidance, (2) teacher education, (3) educational television, and (4) vocational-technical education. Each report was prepared by a task force appointed by the Georgia Nuclear Advisory Commission's committee on manpower and education. Useful for its consideration of needs and issues in each of the four areas.

McDonald, Thomas F. *An Investigation of the Effects of a Rapid Transition from "Open-Door" to "Selective" Admissions*. Doctoral Dissertation, Michigan State University, 1966.

A comparative study of Georgia State before-and-after its selective admissions program in 1959. Covers a six-year period in which the institution made radical revisions in its admission standards and altered its traditional mission and role. Changes in student characteristics were more evident than changes in faculty expectations and grading patterns.

Junior College Act of 1958. No. 53 (House Bill No. 686). General Acts and Resolutions, Volume I: Georgia Laws 1958 Session.

An act to provide for a system of junior colleges in Georgia and defining "junior college" as a community educational institution constructed and operated by a local operation authority (i.e., city, county, or independent school systems).

Pierson, Mary Bynum. *Graduate Work in the South*. Chapel Hill: University of North Carolina Press, 1947.

Contains valuable information about the late development of graduate education in southern universities. Includes useful information about graduate work at the University of Georgia, Emory, Mercer, and Georgia Tech, such as requirements for master's and doctoral degrees, growth of libraries, etc. The first two doctorates at the University of Georgia were conferred in 1940 (one in history and one in education).

Range, Willard. *The Rise and Progress of Negro Colleges in Georgia: 1865-1949*. Athens: University of Georgia Press, 1951.

An informative review of the development of colleges for blacks in Georgia, with good coverage of the institutions in the Atlanta University Complex, Paine College in Augusta, and the three state colleges in Albany, Savannah, and Fort Valley. Depicts the long struggle to overcome the neglect of the state and the general public. Especially good in showing the influence and support of philanthropists and foundations.

Strayer, George D. (Director). *A Report of a Survey of the University System of Georgia*. Atlanta: USGA, 1949.

The third survey conducted by outside experts since 1932; contract was with George Strayer, former director of the Division of Field Studies of the Institute of Educational Research, Teachers College, and thus, numerous references since 1949 to "the Strayer Report."

CHAPTER FOUR
GROWTH AND EXPANSION: 1960-1972

Bowen, Joel Thomas, Jr. *Room To Grow: A Historical Analysis of the Physical Growth at The University of Georgia: 1785-1990.* Doctoral Dissertation, University of Georgia, 1990.

An informative study of the University of Georgia's physical growth. Discusses the geographical and architectural development of the institution as it acquires new missions and responsibilities. Relates the University's growth to that of higher education within the State and nation.

Denning, Richard G. *A Study of Five Selected State-Supported Four-Year Colleges which have Expanded from Junior Level Institutions: An Analysis of Some Resulting Quantitative Changes.* Doctoral Dissertation, University of Georgia, 1972.

An analysis of institutional changes as the result of escalation from junior college to senior college status. Gives various kinds of information on Augusta, Armstrong State, Columbus, and Georgia Southwestern colleges. Includes Southern Tech, an institution that became a four-year unit of Georgia Tech several years later than the first four colleges.

Fincher, Cameron. *Nursing and Paramedical Personnel In Georgia: A Survey of Supply and Demands.* Atlanta: Georgia State College, 1962.

A thirteen-month study of twelve health professions in the State of Georgia. Employers were surveyed for vacancies, turnover, and future personnel needs; colleges and schools were surveyed for supply of personnel from educational and training programs.

Educating Georgia's People: Investment in the Future. Atlanta: Governor's Commission To Improve Education, 1963.

Final report of the commission appointed by Governor Carl Sanders in 1963. Excellent staff work and exceptional group of consultants, plus remarkable representation of the public interest by a blue-ribbon group, led to recommendations concerning statewide goals, planning, financing, and excellence at all levels of public education.

Martin, S. Walter. *A Role and Scope Study of the University System of Georgia.* (Unpublished manuscript, 1966).

Study prepared with staff assistance from the Institute of Higher Education. In 1966 Dr. Martin was vice chancellor of the University System and president-elect of Valdosta State College.

McGrath, Earl J. *The Predominantly Negro Colleges and Universities in Transition.* New York: Bureau of Publications, Teachers College, Columbia University, 1965.

An excellent study of the historically black colleges in the 1960s. Includes useful information about the institutions, their faculties, facilities, academic programs, and student services. Makes a strong case for institutional support as a national objective and in the public interest.

Regents Study on Community Junior Colleges in Georgia. Report to the Board of Regents. (Preliminary Draft, December 1964).

First draft of the committee's report in which recommendations for Bibb County-Houston County, Downtown Atlanta, West Atlanta, and South Atlanta areas were made. Includes detailed data on high school graduates, population growth, etc.

Simpson, George L., Jr. *A Dam Has Broken*. A Statement of Vital Interest to All Georgians by the Chancellor of the University System of Georgia. Atlanta: University System of Georgia, 1967.

A significant and influential discussion of the University System's need for additional public support in the days of its most rapid growth. The author was chancellor from 1965 to 1978.

System Summary. A Publication of the University System of Georgia.

A monthly summary of activities and events taking place in the University System. First issue was dated November 4, 1964; subsequent issues give particular emphasis to actions, decisions, policies of Regents and to changes in key personnel: Regents, chancellor's staff, presidents, and others. Was changed in 1990 to *The System Supplement*, a smaller, briefer publication.

CHAPTER FIVE
REFORM AND CONSOLIDATION: 1972-1984

Barth, Elizabeth A. *A Study of Academic Programs for Superior Students in Georgia Colleges and Universities*. Doctoral Dissertation, University of Georgia, 1981.

The status of academic programs designed to meet the needs of superior college students in Georgia. Includes the perspectives of directors and coordinators of programs for superior students in terms of program effectiveness and efficiency.

Boardman, Katherine B. *Employer Perceptions of Educational Outcomes from Georgia Colleges.* Doctoral Dissertation, University of Georgia, 1981.

A survey of employer satisfaction with the preparation of Georgia graduates and the extent of corporate participation in higher education considered appropriate for their organizations. Addresses the opportunities for participation in planning of educational programs.

Davis, Margaret C. *A Survey of Community Services Policies, Procedures, and Practices in Institutions of Higher Education in Georgia.* Doctoral Dissertation, University of Georgia, 1981.

The capability and commitment of public and private colleges in Georgia to respond to community educational needs and expectations. Survey found community service to be an objective of most colleges.

The Eighties and Beyond: A Commitment to Excellence. A Report of a Statewide Needs Assessment for Public Higher Education. Atlanta: Board of Regents, University System of Georgia, February 1983.

Based on a statewide needs assessment and identifying quality improvement, accessibility and centralization, effective delivery systems, leadership, productivity, and financial support as the State of Georgia's major needs.

Assessment Resource Book. Staff reports and collected data for Board of Regents' comprehensive statewide needs assessment initiated in 1981. (Atlanta: USGA, 1983).

Fincher, Cameron. *Planning For A Statewide System of Public Higher Education: Fifty Years of Trial, Error, and Eventual Success in Georgia.* Athens: Institute of Higher Education, University of Georgia, 1984.

A paper that covers many of Georgia's earlier efforts to adopt statewide planning for institutional and program development. Emphasizes the difficulties of statewide planning in the post-WWII years.

Fincher, Cameron. *Adult Learners and the SAT in the University System of Georgia.* Athens: Institute of Higher Education, University of Georgia, 1983.

An analysis of the academic performance of 1,694 adult learners in institutions of the University System. Defines adult learners as first-time freshmen who are over 24 years in age. Relates SAT scores and secondary preparation to college grades, age, gender, reasons for attending college, fields of study, and other indices of performance such as credits carried and credit earned.

Fincher, Cameron. "The Adversities of Success: The Responsibilities of Governing Boards in Meeting the Special Needs of Students." A paper presented at the annual meeting of the Association of Governing Boards in San Francisco in April 1984.

Discusses the responsibilities of governing boards for academic policies and standards that address the problems of educationally disadvantaged students. Programs in developmental studies at Savannah State and the University of Georgia are described as exemplary models within a context of systemwide policies.

Fincher, Cameron. *Uses of the SAT in the University System of Georgia.* New York: College Entrance Examination Board (Report No. 86-5), 1986.

A survey of the frequency and effectiveness with which SAT scores are used in advisement and counseling, recruitment and admissions, academic and administrative decision making, research and planning, and developmental studies. Includes abstracts of doctoral dissertations, research reports, etc. dealing with the SAT and a meta-analysis of 26 years of SAT scores, high school averages, and college grades.

Formula For Excellence: Financing Georgia's University System in the '80s. Final Report of the Study Committee on Public Higher Education Finance. Atlanta: Office of the Governor, September 1982.

Recommends differentiated funding of institutions according to mission and functions. Universities, senior colleges, and junior colleges should be funded according to instructional productivity in five major program areas (humanities and social sciences; area studies and applied or professional fields; sciences and technological specialties; remedial/developmental education; and the professions of medicine, dentistry, and veterinary medicine).

Galvin, Marc A. *Policies and Practices for Transfer Credit and Credit-by-Examination in Georgia Postsecondary Institutions.* Doctoral Dissertation, University of Georgia, 1982.

A study of policies and practices concerning transfer credit and credit-by-examination in Georgia postsecondary institutions and how these procedures are instituted.

Governor's Committee on Postsecondary Education:

Postsecondary Issues: Action Agenda for the Eighties. Atlanta: COPE, 1979.

Report issued by the State's second 1202 commission as the result of its charge by Governor George Busbee to identify major problems, issues, and concerns confronting postsecondary education.

Georgia's Postsecondary Education in the Eighties: Goals and Objectives. Atlanta: COPE, 1980.

Second report issued by the Committee as the result of reappointment and a charge by Governor Busbee to identify statewide goals and objectives in postsecondary education.

Georgia Postsecondary Education: Where We Are and Where We Need To Be. Atlanta: COPE, 1981.

The third report issued by the Governor's Commission on Postsecondary Education. Includes efforts to assess progress being made toward the State's postsecondary goals and objectives and reports progress in offering a diversity of institutions and programs, educational opportunities that serve student career needs, and cooperation among postsecondary institutions. Substantial progress was not being made, however, in public awareness, institutional responsiveness to educational needs, and adequate opportunities for a changing clientele.

Maintaining Progress in Georgia: Recommendations for Today and Concerns for Tomorrow. Atlanta: COPE, 1982.

Summarizes the Committee's efforts to identify issues and problems, to identify statewide goals and objectives, and to assess achievement of educational goals. Recommends state policies for student financial aid, college admissions and remedial assistance, geographic access and program planning, and planning for future needs. Among recommendations is the establishment of a statewide advisory commission on postsecondary education.

✤✤✤

Holbrook, Margaret W. *An Analysis of Policies and Programs for Increasing Student Retention in Institutions of Higher Education in Georgia.* Doctoral Dissertation, University of Georgia, 1981.

Surveys policies and programs in Georgia colleges for improving student retention. Describes differences in estimated retention rates which occur at public, private, two-year, and four-year colleges.

New State Directions for Postsecondary Vocational Education. Report of the Vocational Education Task Force (Robert B. Ormsby, Chairman). Atlanta: VETF, 1983.

Report of the task force appointed by Governor Harris to recommend new forms of governance for vocational education that would not require an independent state agency or constitutional authority.

Southern Regional Education Board:

Priorities for Postsecondary Education in the South. Atlanta: SREB, 1976.

Position statement by the SREB giving nine priorities for postsecondary education. Two priorities deal with statewide planning; four deal with needed curricular or program change in postsecondary institutions. The remaining three priorities deal with pervasive problems and issues that require the attention and concern of policy and decision makers at most levels of institutional and public action.

Within Our Reach. Report of the Commission on Goals for Higher Education in the South. Atlanta: SREB, 1961.

An exceptionally influential report that addressed the needs and opportunities for the development of higher education in the South. The goals stated are "optimal but reasonable" and decidedly within reach of the colleges and universities of the southern region.

❖❖❖

Weast, Philip G. *A Profile of Interinstitutional Cooperation Among Public and Private Institutions of Higher Education in Georgia.* Doctoral Dissertation, University of Georgia, 1981.

A study of interinstitutional cooperation among three sectors of higher education in Georgia. Considers areas of cooperation and the effectiveness of cooperation; major reasons for institutional involvement in cooperation; and agencies, associations, and agreements through which most cooperation occurs.

CHAPTER SIX
REVIEW AND COORDINATION: 1984-1990

Albright, John W. High School Courses and College Performance: *A Study of State-Mandated College Preparatory Curriculum Requirements for College Admission.* Doctoral Dissertation, University of Georgia, 1990.

Study was conducted on a sample of 426 freshmen at the University of Georgia and included statistical control of relevant background variables. Found a significant correlation between college grades and completion of the required preparatory curriculum.

Booth, Le-Quita R. *The University System of Georgia's Administrative Development Program: A Means To Increase The Pool of Black Administrators.* Doctoral Dissertation, University of Georgia, 1987.

Addresses the effectiveness of inservice development programs for academic administrators. Based on interviews with participating Regents Fellows, supervising administrators, presidents of participating institutions, and professional staff members who designed and implemented the program. Concludes that program objectives were effectively achieved but important personal and institutional expectations were not realized.

Burge, Lee, Fincher, Cameron, Hooper, John W., and Langdale, Noah. *A Report to the Chancellor: An Assessment of The University System of Georgia (1989)*. Presented to the Board of Regents of the University System of Georgia, 1989.

Report is the result of a two-year assessment of the University System at the request of Chancellor H. Dean Propst. The major thrust of the assessment team was to analyze the causes of difficulties in higher education, and to assess the course of its development.

Improving Undergraduate Teacher Education Programs in Georgia. Recommendations of the External Review Committee for the Improvement of Teacher Education in Georgia. Atlanta: University System of Georgia, 1986.

Report on the recommendations of an external review committee convened to consider teacher education, ways of improving teacher education programs, and actions or studies that should be undertaken. Contains forty-three recommendations for educating teachers.

Morris, Libby V. *Health Professions Personnel in Georgia*. Athens: Institute of Higher Education, University of Georgia, 1987.

A comprehensive statewide needs assessment involving health facilities, educational and training programs, and personnel in thirty-two health occupations. Although Georgia health care has improved significantly since the early 1960s, Georgia is still below the national average in most areas of health care.

Proposal for the Establishment of Regional Universities. Prepared by the Planning and Oversight Committee of the Board of Regents. Atlanta: University System of Georgia (September 13, 1989).

This committee report provides a framework for the consideration of regional universities within the University System. Included are organizational concepts and criteria by which regional universities should be approved. Contains the committee's recommendations and a proposed organizational chart for Georgia Southern University.

Roberts, Derrell C. (Chairman). *Mission and Role of Public Two-year Colleges in Georgia.* (Report of the Study Committee appointed by Chancellor H. Dean Propst in 1987).

A survey of the varied mission and roles of public two-year colleges, as perceived by their presidents and other institutional leaders. Documents at least five major roles that two-year colleges actively play in providing educational services to their constituencies.

Subcommittee on Academic Degree Program Assessment. *Academic Degree Program Assessment in the University System of Georgia: A Tentative Statement of Rationale, Purposes, and Procedures.* Prepared for the Administrative Advisory Committee (July 1977).

Foreshadows much of the later concern with the assessment of educational outcomes. Discusses problems of definition, measurement and assessment, purposes and expected outcomes of assessment, and the diversity of instruments and techniques available to program heads and other institutional leaders.

The University System of Georgia: Planning for the 1990s. Atlanta: Board of Regents of the University System of Georgia, 1990.

Report on a two-year, long-range planning study involving the 34 institutions of the University System. States the mission of the University System, its goals and objectives for the 1990s, and the institutional roles of universities, senior colleges, and two-year colleges. Based on consideration of demographic and economic trends, statewide and regional needs, and an assessment of needs in the major programs of the System. Recommendations address increased participation in higher education, strengthening the University System's role in economic development, coordinating institutional roles, and improving the quality of institutional programs and services.

CHAPTER SEVEN
STATUS AND POTENTIAL: 1990-2000

Almanac of Higher Education 1991. Prepared by Editors of the Chronicle of Higher Education. Chicago: University of Chicago Press, 1991.

An outstanding source of information on public and private higher education. Published annually as a special supplement in the *Chronicle* and then as a paperback volume for commercial distribution. Especially useful for its summary of national statistics and its profiles of the fifty states.

Carnegie Foundation for the Advancement of Teaching. *A Classification of Institutions of Higher Education.* Princeton: CFAT, 1987.

A functional classification of institutions in terms of educational level, degree programs, and resources. Classifies research universities, doctorate-granting institutions, comprehensive universities and colleges, and liberal arts colleges at two levels (I and II). Other classifications include two-year colleges, and professional institutions.

❖❖❖

Fincher, Cameron and Bachtel, Douglas C. "Higher Education in Georgia: A System Profile." Athens: *Issues Facing Georgia* Series, Cooperative Extension Service, University of Georgia (June 1991).

A study of enrollments in public colleges and universities by county of student origin. Includes institutional enrollment patterns for universities, senior colleges, and two-year colleges as well as expenditures on higher education by state and local government.

Hudson, Cathy Mayes and Pounds, Haskins R. *Improving Preparation for College: The Effects of the College Preparation Curriculum On Academic Success in the University System of Georgia: 1988-1990.* Atlanta: Board of Regents of the University System of Georgia (June 1991).

An excellent summary of data collected in a study of the college preparation curriculum (CPC) approved by the Regents in 1984 for implementation in 1988. Provides data on institutions by subject matter field for the years 1988, 1989, and 1990. Concludes that the recommended high school curriculum is effective in preparing students for college but suggests that the percent of high school students completing the CPC is *not* increasing.

Information Digest 1989-1990: Public Higher Education in Georgia. Atlanta: Office of Research and Planning, University System of Georgia (April 1990).

An invaluable source of information on students, faculties, finances, and facilities within the University System. Includes general information on the University System and its institutions. First issued in 1984 and continued annually since that time.

Marks, Joseph L. *SREB Fact Book On Higher Education 1990.*
Atlanta: Southern Regional Education Board, 1990.

The latest in a twenty-year series of factbooks giving comparable data and information on higher education in the SREB states. Includes comparable data for the nation and provides a profile of higher education in Georgia as well as other southern states. An excellent source of information since the early 1960s.

Marks, Joseph L. *Georgia: Public College and University Faculty Salaries Compared to National and SREB Averages: 1990-91.*
Atlanta: Southern Regional Education Board, 1991.

An occasional report on faculty salaries in the public colleges and universities of Georgia. Comparisons are for full-time faculty members by institutional classification without regard for faculty rank or field of specialization. Other reports in the series deal with faculty salaries in other states.

Pounds, Haskin and Anderson, Robert S. *Normative Data for the 1989-1990 Freshman Class.* Atlanta: Office of Research and Planning, University System of Georgia, 1991.

The thirty-third issue of the University System's annual norms booklet for SAT scores, high school averages, and freshman grades. Printed in a new format with institutional profiles and norms that contain excellent information on the status and quality of public education in Georgia.

APPENDIX
The Constitutional Authority of the Board of Regents

The authority and responsibilities of the University System of Georgia Board of Regents derive from the Constitution of the State of Georgia, as revised and approved in the 1982 general election. The authority and powers granted by the State Constitution are as follows:

PARAGRAPH I. *University System of Georgia; board of regents.* (a) There shall be a Board of Regents of the University System of Georgia which shall consist of one member from each congressional district in the state and five additional members from the state at large, appointed by the Governor and confirmed by the Senate. The Governor shall not be a member of said board. The members in office on June 30, 1983, shall serve out the remainder of their respective terms. As each term of office expires, the Governor shall appoint a successor as herein provided. All such terms of members shall be for seven years. Members shall serve until their successors are appointed and qualified. In the event of a vacancy on the board by death, resignation, removal, or any reason other than the expiration of a member's term, the Governor shall fill such vacancy; and the person so appointed shall serve until confirmed by the Senate and, upon confirmation, shall serve for the unexpired term of office.

(b) The board of regents shall have the exclusive authority to create new public colleges, junior colleges, and universities in the State of Georgia, subject to approval by majority vote in the House of Representatives and the Senate. Such vote shall not be required to change

161

the status of a college, institution or university existing on the effective date of this Constitution. The government, control, and management of the University System of Georgia and all of the institutions in said system shall be vested in the Board of Regents of the University System of Georgia.

(c) All appropriations made for the use of any or all institutions in the university system shall be paid to the board of regents in a lump sum, with the power and authority in said board to allocate and distribute the same among the institutions under its control in such way and manner and in such amounts as will further an efficient and economical administration of the university system.

(d) The board of regents may hold, purchase, lease, sell, convey, or otherwise dispose of public property, execute conveyances thereon, and utilize the proceeds arising therefrom; may exercise the power of eminent domain in the manner provided by law; and shall have such other powers and duties as provided by law.

(e) The board of regents may accept bequests, donations, grants, and transfers of land, buildings, and other property for the use of the University System of Georgia.

(f) The qualifications, compensation, and removal from office of the members of the board of regents shall be as provided by law (*Constitution of the State of Georgia,* Article VIII, Section IV).

Index

About the Author

Dr. Cameron Fincher is Regents Professor of Higher Education and Psychology at the University of Georgia and has been Director of the Institute of Higher Education since 1969. In September 1946 he enrolled in the Day Division of the University System Center and since that time, with the exception of one year while earning his master's degree, he has been either a student or a faculty member in the University System of Georgia. He was a student at the University System Center when it became the Atlanta Division of the University of Georgia and a faculty member when the Atlanta Division became Georgia State College.

His graduate degrees were earned at the University of Minnesota (MA, 1951) and Ohio State University (PhD, 1956) where he majored in psychology. In 1951 he was appointed instructor and counselor at the Atlanta Division where he taught psychology and established the Office of Testing and Counseling. In 1965 he transferred to the University of Georgia in Athens where he was first associate director (1965-1969) and then director of the Institute of Higher Education. In his work at the Institute Dr. Fincher has actively participated in all phases of institutional and program planning, development, assessment, and evaluation.

In 1957 he was appointed to the first of many statewide or systemwide committees on which he has served. Since that time he has worked closely with the Board of Regents and other state agencies in the development and improvement of higher education in Georgia. From 1978 to 1983 he was a member of the Governor's Committee on Postsecondary Education, and from 1984 through 1988 he was actively involved in the Regents Administrative Development Program for minority faculty members. Over the years he has also worked closely with the Southern Regional Education Board, the Southern Education Foundation, the College Board, Educational Testing Service, the Southern Association of Colleges and Schools, and other regional or national agencies concerned with research and development in higher education.

The author's interest in the historical development of the University System began in the early 1950s when its central offices were located in the same building with the Atlanta Division. That interest continues to be whetted by numerous opportunities to explain the University System to doctoral students in higher education, to visiting educators from other countries—and to faculty colleagues across campus.

About the Institute

The Institute of Higher Education was established in 1964 in response to the Southern Regional Education Board's recommendation that one or more universities in the region should establish a center or institute for the study of higher education. The Institute's original charges were: to help recruit and develop faculty members for institutions of higher education in Georgia, to conduct institutional studies for the University of Georgia, and to cooperate with other educational agencies and institutions in the development of higher education within the state and the region.

The Institute staff is actively involved in many projects and activities related to the overall development of higher education and to the improvement of institutions, programs, and services. Closely related to all Institute activities is a doctoral program specifically developed for the study of undergraduate, graduate, and professional education. In addition to the doctoral program the Institute staff has maintained a special interest in administrative leadership, faculty development, instructional improvement, program assessment, and the legal issues of American higher education. More recently the mission of the Institute includes commitment to the continuing professional education of academic administrators, professional staff members, and college teachers.

Throughout its twenty-seven years of service, the Institute has continued to work closely with the Southern Regional Education Board and other national or regional organizations concerned with the development of higher education. In particular, the Institute has worked closely with the Board of Regents, the Chancellor's staff, and other state agencies dealing with the improvement of education in Georgia.